SERVING GOD BY SERVING OTHERS

Other Books by Fr. Michael Briese

Reflections of a Life Lived in Christ

Charismata

Rich and Poor: Seeking the Common Good by Striving to Build Up the Kingdom of God

A Life in Christ

Works of Mercy and Service

Gift of Prayer: The Language of the Human Heart

Serving Our Sisters and Brothers

Seeds for a Holy Life

Dedication

Dedicated to the very people whose hearts are blessed with an abundance of God's love. May they always be blessed with a heartfelt desire, the gifts and abilities needed, and the willingness to go out into the world and imitate Christ by serving our brothers and sisters. May they forever strive to imitate Christ by serving the poor, weak, suffering, doubtful and those among our most vulnerable neighbors and strangers. May all such dedicated modern disciples of Christ be blessed every day with everlasting joy, greater faith, lifelong perseverance, a message of inclusion and greater love.

Table of Contents

DISCIPLESHIP OF CHRIST

May the holiness of our good and gracious Lord continue to permeate the very depths of your being. May you, as a faithful modern disciple of Christ, continue to journey throughout the passing of each day with a keen and attentive awareness of Christ's presence. Our good Lord comes into our daily lives all so often in the simple words expressed by a child, in the wise guidance provided to us by our elders and also often in words we hear from a person who enters into our life for just a brief time…maybe just a few minutes. Be attentive to your own life. Look around and creation presents the invaluable treasures granted unto you and countless others. If you do not look, you will not see. If you do not listen, you will not hear. As a modern disciple of Christ, our dearly beloved Lord speaks to you and often through you on a daily basis. Do you give time to our Lord on a daily basis?

Can you say with certainty that deep within the soft stillness contained within your own being there rests our Savior? Can you see what others see? Can you understand within the very depths of your being that our Lord is with you? Inside you are the gifts of faith, of believing and knowing. Do you cherish what God gives you every day? Do you believe that angels breathe, and that love will live on? Are you bound up in a close relationship with our Lord? Do you fully understand He is but a breath away from where you are? Do you really KNOW He is with you now and until the hour of your death? Do you understand and grasp that your faith is that resilient spiritual power that was placed within the very depths of your divinely endowed human spirit at that sacred moment of your conception and sustained at that holy moment when your sacred, precious and holy birth occurred?

You are a modern disciple of our dear Lord. Dare yourself to pick up the Cross and run with it! Do this on a daily basis. Be certain you will suffer. You will fall and be tripped, and you will be thrown down. But, when you fall or are thrown down, all in the name of Christ, it is then, at such moments in your life, when you will be lifted up and carried through those tough moments and times in life. You will discover the suffering that life will thrust on every person. And you can discover there in such moments the great strength that only our Lord can provide. You will become blessed with more and more faith, hope, love, courage, perseverance, prudence, knowledge, understanding and wisdom. As you venture through each hour of each passing day, you will be blessed with a greater awareness of our Lord's presence. You will become more blessed with greater heartfelt wisdom, and the goodness and wise counsel of the Holy Spirit. It is written, "They that hope in the Lord will renew their strength, they will soar on eagles' wings, They will run and not grow weary, walk and not grow faint" (Isa. 40:31). Do this and you shall be a disciple of Christ. AMEN.

July 7, 2019

GOOD SAMARITAN

Always, always remember: Jesus said, "You shall love the Lord, your God, with all your heart, with all your being, with all your strength, and with all your mind, and your neighbor as yourself." This ancient guidance from our Savior reminds you, me and all who seek Truth, that we have people to care for, people to feed, people to help and guide and even people who need to be loved. All these and so many other countless people will enter into your life at times when you least expect them. They, to a large degree, will be strangers to you. Even today, right now, there are countless people whose lives you will be able to help, guide and inform. Always imitate the ancient Good Samaritan. Be there for those in need. One day, you will be in need and some strangers will help you along the way. And they will help you, not for money, but rather because their hearts, minds and spirits are already keenly aware of Christ's presence in their daily lives.

There resting within the very depths of your being rests the Holy Spirit. This Divine gift is exactly what calls YOU to reach out and be willing to serve others…including a stranger in need. One day, you will be a stranger in the midst of other people. They will not know you and you will not know them. You will need their help. They have no obligation to care for you… you are nothing but a stranger in their midst. Still, you will breathe deeply hoping, praying that someone will come and help!

It happens in one's life. If this has not already happened, I promise, before you die, you, too, will come to see the hands of God working in your daily life. If you do not look, you will not see. If you do not listen, you will not hear. Seek our Lord. Be attentive. Be open to change. Be or become a Good Samaritan willing to serve strangers in need. One day, Good Samaritans will enter briefly into your life. That will be a time when the Divine already had spoken to humanity.

Samaritans and Jews could not stand one another. They had great hatred and animosity toward one another. For a Samaritan to help a Jew was forbidden. Read this Scripture story and you will be wowed! Live out this Good Samaritan story and you will have chosen to live out a devout and holy life.

In your ongoing pursuit for Truth, never give up. Be a modern disciple with a heart afire and the wisdom of an elderly man. At the end of each day, when you have paid for almost nothing, be humbled by the immense blessings God has given to you. Last, may all of us give thanks to our dear God. AMEN.

July 14, 2019

MARTHA AND MARY

The widely known Bible story about the two sisters, Martha and Mary, is a great classic story about family relationships, our relationships with members of our fellow parishioners and people in our local communities. Are you more of a Martha? Or are you more like Mary? My own answer with regard to my lifelong journey in search of Christ, greater faith and knowledge and even the ways I choose to live out the Gospel in my daily life is that all of us are called to live out the Gospel message by sometimes being more like Martha and other times being more like Mary.

This need to make time to ask and learn about our faith, our own faith journey, and life require times when we just STOP! We go off and in silence, prayer and faith, we pray. Prayer is the language of the human heart. Love is the greatest gift and human capacity each person has.

There is a time for everything: A time to be still and in that stillness, ask our dear Lord to speak to your open heart, an open mind and open spirit. In stillness and silence, pray NOT by saying words, but rather by listening. Listen with your prayerful heart and in silence and quietude know our dear Lord speaks to you. Listen! Listen in prayer! After we are able to pray, we as Christians, and modern disciples of our Risen Lord Jesus Christ, also know we are to live out our daily faith by putting our faith into action. This is what Mary exemplifies, and Martha is also right.

Martha's example is sustained in the following words found in James 2:15–17, "If a brother or sister has nothing to wear and has no food for the day, and one of you says to them, 'Go in peace, keep warm, and eat well,' but you do not give them the necessities of the body, what good is it? So also, faith of itself, if it does not have works, is dead." Our dear Lord has smiled on us and blessed us in countless ways. Martha is a great example of the Christian whose heart is in the right place. Martha is a disciple who strives to live out her faith in Christ by serving others in very concrete ways. She exemplifies our faith by putting her faith into action and thus living out the Gospel. However, staying busy by itself is not the whole answer.

Mary is also correct in that the modern disciple of Christ, who is constantly serving Christ by serving others, also needs to make time to go off and do nothing. It is time to be still and in silence simply remain still, find rest, and an abundance of God's many graces. With a prayerful spirit and an open heart listen as our dear Lord ever so softly provides Divine wisdom, Divine mercy and Divine counsel. This is time to imitate Mary by resting in the company of Christ, and opening one's heart, mind and spirit to Christ. Wonder and you find wisdom. Pray and you will see God.

July 21, 2019

ASK, SEEK, AND KNOCK

Jesus said, "And I tell you, ask and you will receive; seek and you will find; knock and the door will be opened to you. For everyone who asks, receives; and the one who seeks, finds; and to the one who knocks, the door will be opened" (Luke 11:9–10). Our good Lord is with you and all people whose hearts are in search of our beloved Lord. Our Lord is a Lord from which we can freely choose to learn. He is our God whose infinite love, Divine mercy and undeserved compassion permeate billions of daily lives, attuned hearts and keen minds. Overall our beloved Father calls out to you and me, and all whose hearts are restless and in search of greater Truth, understanding and God.

Sometimes in our lives a distant relative, a long-lost friend or even a stranger knocks at our door as they seek maybe a new, fresh or greater understanding about some old family event, or maybe something that occurred long ago at work, or simply to refresh their own understanding about you and where you are at now, at this point in your life. They come into our midst and we are not even sure as to WHY they are now in our midst. Why? What are they asking from me? Can I really help this old friend, acquaintance or relative? If so, HOW? All these are reasonable questions to ask.

Believe me, when a long-lost person who once was a part of your life steps up to ask you for help, greater clarity or greater understanding, then you try to do what Christ would do. And that is to welcome the person, meet them where they are and listen very, very carefully to their words and the points of their words. Do not hesitate to ask them for greater clarity. Do all this with an open heart, a keen and attentive mind and a spirit of compassion and mercy.

Life does throw its curves. Sometimes such events occur in very unexpected ways. When they do happen, strive to see a fellow human being in a time of need, a need for greater clarity, understanding and justice. Be patient. Listen carefully. Be attentive. Extend your sincere hospitality by welcoming them. Be practical. Do not judge them or their lives. Do all this in a sincere way, and this is exactly what our Lord Jesus would ask us to do.

Be or become a person whose heart is like that of our Lord Jesus' Sacred Heart. Understand that moments such as these are times when our dear Holy Spirit awakens you, your heart and your mind. As a modern disciple of Christ, be patient, listen, and strive to imitate our dear Lord. Ask and it shall be given. Seek and you will find. Knock and the door will be opened. May we strive to sincerely live our daily lives in the footsteps and imitation of our dear Lord Jesus Christ. And may we do so in love. AMEN.

July 28, 2019

RICH MAN AND POVERTY OF HEART

God spoke to the rich man and said, "'You fool, this night your life will be demanded of you; and the things you have prepared, to whom will they belong?' Thus will it be for the one who stores up treasure for himself but is not rich in what matters to God" (Luke 12:20). Since ancient days, humanity has always clearly understood that one's life, one's relationship to fellow human beings and God will never be judged by the acquisition of wealth, power or one's asset–liability ratio. The ancient prophets all too often had to remind the Jewish people about this absolute truth.

Today in our modern society, all too many who claim to be "good" people, "fair" people and "honest people go out every day and their primary desire is to end this day, this week, this month richer than they were on the first of the month. Well, maybe it's time to reread this great Bible story found in Luke 12:13–21. Materials, things, mere objects will never bring happiness, peace or love to one's heart. Never!

In my lifetime I have met many people who are rich and yet they suffer a deep sense of impoverishment in their relationships with their family members, old friends, and even many other people they have met in life. Too often they just "use" people and afterward discard "those people" like an old piece of equipment. Owning farmland, shopping centers, office buildings, stocks or other financial investments cannot bring the heartfelt peace most members of the human race desire. This already has been borne out by the rate of drug and alcohol addiction, suicide and habitual immoral or unethical behaviors that exist in families whose houses can be found near the top of a beautiful hill or built back on land hidden away and out of view from the community main streets or along the base of beautiful mountainous terrain.

What is worth more to you? Maybe some bigger barns bursting with a great abundance of harvested crops or maybe the deep abiding love you have for your parents, your spouse, your children, your closest friends, the neighbor down the road or even the stranger? Which is worth more? Our culture will always answer with a strong, clearly resonating shout of financial wealth! Yes! Wealth certainly brings greater power, influence, and choices. No doubt! That has been, is now and probably always will be humanity's favorite choice!

St. Luke reminds us that this is a fool's choice. The greatest assets you possess are God-given. Seek truth within. Search in prayer and your heartfelt wisdom will bless you in many ways. In the end, the rich will die, and they like the poor will simply be fitted into a casket, buried amid mere poor folk, and just like the poor, they too will have mere worms and bugs as their immediate neighbors. Rich or poor we all go from dust to dust and ashes to ashes. Which is more important to you…a life abundant with love or a life spent in acquiring more and more things? Your life is a sacred, precious and holy life. You have a place and a role to play in the unfolding of God's Kingdom.

August 4, 2019

THE GREATEST TREASURE

Not so deep within you rests the greatest treasure! There within the silence of your heart is a sacred place, a holy presence and as St. Paul writes, therein is a temple for our dear Lord. Take some time daily to walk away from the noises of the day. Ignore the countless distractions. Avoid loudness, for each day can too often impose its own vexations. Daily noises and other distractions take us ever more distant from the very presence of our Lord right within the silence of a human heart. Give some time each day to our Lord. Do this in memory of our God's only begotten Son, whose death on that ancient Cross brought you, me and the human race the promise of eternal life hereafter.

Certainly, you hear, and I hear, so many who simply mock the very idea of God and even religion overall. Let those who mock and jeer have the last laugh. Let them. If that reflects their own lives, then make some time to pray for them. Pray that the Holy Spirit will enkindle their heart, mind and spirit with greater faith, hope and love. Always be willing and able to pray for those who might not think like you, live like you or believe like you. Regardless of such differences, I have to believe that you and maybe even some of them might understand… maybe even believe the words you could share with them. Just say to them in a sincere manner, "Your life is a holy life, a sacred life and a precious life. It is precisely because God has created you out of Divine love and in His image and likeness that God has a role for you to play in the unfolding of His kingdom here at hand." Share this part of the Good News. This is what our Lord asks of us. Be gentle, understanding and kind. Share the Good News of Jesus Christ even if they laugh at you or mock you.

Our Lord came among us to serve us. Jesus did not come to be served by us. Living out the Gospel is not always going to be easy, comfortable or without its challenges and even burdens. Still, the Gospel message has consistently throughout human history, since the ancient times of the Roman Empire, provided billions of lives with countless blessings, greater faith and many, many ways in which generations after generations have ever more fully heard, embraced and lived out the Gospel of Jesus Christ.

Humanity has ever so slowly learned HOW to live out the Gospel. Nations, tribes, ethnic groups and races have grown in our common human capacities to let go of the past, to love and forgive our enemies, and to live each and every day as God's day (since God provides us with each breaking dawn). The Gospel message reminds us to be deeply appreciative and thankful for every breath we have ever taken. We are invited to more fully understand and humbly acknowledge, that we are breathing now, at this moment, and thus are able to experience the purely granted and unearned gift of human life. God is with us, now, and until the end of time. Blessed are they who walk humbly in the company of Christ.

August 11, 2019

GOD'S FIRE OF LOVE

God's fire of love is cast down into the very depth of your own being. God created YOU out of Divine love and in His image and likeness. He grants you, me and all humanity the finite time of our lives. Every minute and hour of every past day, today and every day to come is a purely unearned gift from God. Within every depth of your own sacred heart is a temple, a place of rest, peace and consolation. Therein rests our dear Lord.

Do not fall to the foolish encouragement that often comes from others, corporations and even our public agencies. They might encourage you to pursue your personal happiness through products or services you can buy, sell, rent, enjoy or own. Your greatest personal "asset" is YOU and what YOU bring out every day when you enter into your part of the world and in particular your place in society. The greatest value you or any human being possesses comes NOT from THINGS you might own, lease or render unto others. No! Go look in a mirror, and there is a reflection of YOU! YOU are one of God's most precious, sacred and holy gifts. YOU are precisely because God has a role for YOU to play in the unfolding of His kingdom here at hand. What is that role? That's a question only YOU can ever hope to learn, understand, pursue and successfully fulfill. Only YOU can live out your lifelong part in helping to build up the kingdom of God here at hand.

At times, when we speak about or hear the word *fire* associated with the Bible, we might think about someone preaching *fire and brimstone*. More often than not, the word *fire* in the Bible symbolizes the blazing and brightly shining radiant love that God freely gives to all whose hearts search for His beloved Son, our Savior Jesus Christ. In this lifetime YOU and all of us owe our own self Truth. We will never find Truth if we bet mostly on the games, things, toys and pleasures our society tells us we MUST have! Do not fall for this approach! It is all a sales pitch! Nothing more! YOU and every human being are worth so much more than any THING on this great planet! Inside of YOU is a heart, hopefully on fire with faith, hope, love and so many other Divine blessings.

May you and your life always be deeply seeded in, and attuned to, our dear Lord. Do unto others as Christ would do. Respect your fellow human beings. May YOU become more keenly aware and able to understand more fully that our Lord, Christ, can be discovered in the eyes of our elders, the deeply flawed lives of the homeless, the lives lived by so many who are severely disabled. In addition, make time for a brutally honest self-examination of how YOU are living out this one God-given life YOU now possess. Gratitude, giving back, countless lifelong daily blessings, creation, every breath you take, the abilities to walk, see, hear, speak and understand…even these are all unearned gifts from God. YOU are blessed this very hour and will be on every day to come. May heartfelt peace and a spirit of awe and thanksgiving permeate your heart, mind and soul. Last, may you, me and all people be humbled by God's fire of love and His countless blessings.

August 18, 2019

THINGS AND KINGS

You have been purchased at a price! Always be willing to humbly recognize and understand that God so loved the world that He sent forth His only begotten Son to preach and teach, to heal and raise from the dead, and to die and rise in fulfilment of the ancient prophets. Be humbled by this eternal example of Divine mercy, Divine compassion and Divine justice. If you doubt this great historical event that transformed human history, then, be brutally honest with yourself and accept His Divine invitation to draw near, to come closer, and to find rest in the company of our dear Lord. Accept this Divine invitation this and every day for the rest of your frail, broken and finite lifetime. Do this and you will come to discover and rediscover the transformative impact Christ will have on you throughout your lifetime. Otherwise, you can choose to put your faith into things or maybe kings.

Your own life has been a sacred, precious and holy life since inception, throughout conception and right up to that hour when God granted you your first breath and the beginning of your one lifetime. You did nothing to earn or merit this treasured gift of human life. Now that you are among us and in this world and of this world, well, what are you giving back to others and our dear Creator? What are you doing NOT necessarily for your own sake, but rather, to help, assist, or guide other people? Are you serving others in a spirit of giving to others in an unconditional manner? Or, when you give, do you give expecting some sort of return?

Learn to give unconditionally. Learn to give even when you do not wish to give. Ask not what others can do for you or your own benefit. Rather, ask what you can do for others. Seek a frank and clear self-examination, and the willingness to pick up your Cross, as did Christ, and to live a daily life with the Gospel as its foundation. Always strive to freely, knowingly and deliberately imitate Christ on a daily basis.

Take this road throughout your lifetime and you will be able to honestly recognize and humbly acknowledge all those events when you thought you had failed, fallen short or might have gotten the situation all wrong. Be humbled by these times and events in your one lifetime. Then humbly acknowledge and be grateful for our dear Lord, the Risen Christ was right there at your side. Such moments in your lifetime will be remembered not for success, but rather for the humbling self-realization that our dear Lord was there at your side, saw you fall, picked you up and carried you through those dark times. Our Lord waits for you now and until the hour of your death. Will you accept this Divine invitation? The choice is yours to make. Otherwise, you can rely on things and kings.

August 25, 2019

A BANQUET FOR
THE BLESSED POOR

"When you hold a banquet, invite the poor, the crippled, the lame, the blind; blessed indeed will you be because of their inability to repay you. For you will be repaid at the resurrection of the righteous" (Luke 14:13–14). These sacred words of Divine mercy, Divine justice and Divine love are ancient heartfelt treasures to be read and then to be lived out one day at a time. Love will always be the greatest gift, the greatest power and the greatest ability you or any human being can ever hope to fathom, develop and live out. You have been invited by our dear Lord and Savior Jesus Christ to draw near, come closer and enter into a lifelong faith-filled love relationship. Are you willing to accept His Divine invitation? This is the question right now: How are you going to answer this Divine invitation?

You have been granted this one lifetime. You did nothing to earn or merit this Divine gift. Certainly, the birth process of human life and your actual delivery into this world came as a pure unconditional gift. God willed you and your gift of life and has done so with no terms or conditions attached. As a human being you have an innate, God-given dignity. You have been granted this one sacred, precious and holy life. How are you going to give unto others as God has given unto you? What are your gifts, talents and skills that you can use to give unto others as others have given unto you?

Many people who are rich in material goods or holdings are so poor in their capacity, willingness and abilities to give unto the least among us. Too often those rich in wealth, power or knowledge are unwilling to acknowledge in a humble and genuine spirit their own countless gifts with which God has blessed them. On the superficial level they appear rich. Yet inside they too often suffer an immense spiritual poverty. They are poor in spirit, blind to Christ's eternal message of New Life in Christ, and crippled in their compassion, concern toward and willingness to serve the least among us.

This spiritual poverty can only be overcome when one is willing to place God as the first, top priority in one's own life and the lives of his or her family members. Blessed are impoverished lives whose faith-filled hearts are blessed with a great spiritual abundance of faith, hope and love.

For both the rich and the poor it is written, "It is in giving that we receive." This gift of your one lifetime holds with it the eternal promise that our Lord is with us. Also, our dear beloved Father who art in heaven asks us to forgive those who trespass against us. In return, we ask our Father to "lead us not into temptation but deliver us from evil." These ancient words provide a map as to HOW to live out a devout life. Consider yourself served this Divine invitation! HOW will you respond? Let all of us, rich or poor, be humbled by this eternal Divine invitation to enter more fully, more closely into the company of Christ. How will you live out your one lifetime? According to your own ways or the Way of Christ?

September 2, 2019

HUMAN DIGNITY

Human dignity, your own personal dignity and that of every other human being, comes NOT from government, one's social status, political powers, corporate assets/liabilities or military might! No! Read Genesis and you will discover that God created Adam and Eve out of Divine love and in His image and likeness. A vast majority of the great saints lived their lives by following along the pathway blazed by our Lord and Savior Jesus Christ. Countless men, women and children were mere peasants and a strong majority of our saints. Most of our martyrs were extremely poor people. Hundreds of thousands, maybe even millions of them, were more often than not illiterate, powerless, so often sick and suffering, and one might even say they were insignificant in terms of the unfolding of human history.

Your own life is a pure gift! The moment of your conception when God breathed human nature and life into you, your life was sealed with Divine love. You and every single person were granted our one common thread—our common human nature—and with that Divine blessing, your life became a sacred, precious and holy life. Each person also has free will. How do you consciously give thanks to God for granting you this one lifetime? Your innate dignity has not been earned by you, or any other person, or concern. Rather your innate dignity rests inside your very being—there within the very depths of your humanity. Be or become a person who is deeply aware and is moved by the presence of our Lord within the very fiber of your being. And be humbled by the human dignity breathed into you and freely given to you by our Creator.

All too often the very wealthy, politically influential and powerful in a society know full well that the ancient proven way of oppressing a nation and its peoples is to divide them, rather than unite the various peoples. Today this divisive strategy is brutally clear to anyone who takes the time to look back at our national history. It is true that history repeats itself. It's NOT exactly the same, but similar to the past, as history repeats itself. Today in our local communities, across our nation and around the world, we see and hear a consistent increase in the ways and rationales used to achieve human divisiveness, arguments regarding human superiority and inferiority, and explanations as to why this people is owed this or that. These very successful strategies in our current society echo past historical circumstances here in our society. Will your heart, mind and spirit freely and knowingly choose to follow in the footsteps of Christ and His eternal Spirit of love and forgiveness? Or will you fall like a fool to the ongoing efforts to "divide and conquer" human beings? I pray, and I ask you to pray that we, as children of God, fellow human beings, can once again rediscover and grow in our daily efforts to love others, including our neighbors, strangers and even our enemies. Let us recognize and sustain the dignity of all human beings. Then pray for peace in ALL human hearts.

September 8, 2019

PRODIGAL CHILDREN

You and I are among the worldwide brotherhood and sisterhood of God's prodigal children. Luke's widely known story about the prodigal son speaks ever so clearly to countless people. One need not be a Christian, Jew or a member of any other faith. Rather, we are members of a universal nature, a universal creation, and a universal brokenness. By the time we enter into the last third of life, we—by accident or maybe by our own due diligence—have come to discover and address our own limitations, frailties, imperfections and mistakes. Like the ancient prodigal son, every person including you and I walking this planet can see and recognize our mere, imperfect and frail humanity. We do good things. We do bad things. We have talents and skills. We have so many things we cannot understand, or do, but still at which one truly can succeed. We see the speck in the eyes of others and then humbly acknowledge the speck in our own eyes. Life can be a great teacher, more so than even a classroom. As a prodigal child of God, you have been granted a lifetime. Your personal happiness or sense of purpose will never be found inside a liquor bottle, or through some drug, or in your accumulation of toys such as houses, farms, businesses or any other THINGS! No, you, as a prodigal and greatly imperfect and broken human being will ultimately come to discover true happiness, peace and purpose within the silence of your own heart. Go there! Now! Do not hesitate. Do not put off until tomorrow what you can do today. Go in prayer and amid silence, enter more fully into prayer— the language of the human heart. Go there and amid that stillness you will evermore fully grasp the presence of our dear Lord. Right there… inside you, within the very depths of your heart is a temple…a holy place…a quiet place…a place in which our dear beloved Lord finds rest.

We are our Creator's prodigal sons and daughters. God has breathed life into you and all humanity. Most people are good people. Some are bad. Some people are even evil! But there, somewhere out there, right there in your own self rests the Divine. Whether you are more good, bad or a balanced mixture of both good and bad, seek a quiet place. In that quietude, be still. In that stillness, close your eyes, say nothing, breathe slowly, and allow your own spirit to find stillness and rest. In that moment, worry not about yourself, anyone else or anything. Leave out the problems of the world. Be still. In those holy moments our dear Lord will speak in you, to you and ultimately through you. There amid that rest, your spiritual awareness will grow and over a lifetime will mature. Do NOT say to yourself or anyone else that you cannot do this! That kind of thought of self-discouragement can be the work of the evil one. Rather, if you really think you cannot pray, then, ask our dear Lord to bless you with the trust of a child and the wisdom of our elders.

Trust. Believe. Seek Truth. Strive to live out the Gospel by putting your faith into action. Persevere! Never give up! Do this even in those times when it just might not make sense to you. Still, believe, and go forward. You as a prodigal child of God are already a blessed imperfect sinner. Our Father will always welcome you into His company. Come home to our Father. Do this in the Holy Name of His only begotten Son, our Lord and Savior Jesus Christ. Then give thanks to God and be at peace.

September 15, 2019

GOD AND MAMMON

No one can serve two masters. He will either hate one and love the other, or be devoted to one and despise the other. You cannot serve God and mammon." (Matt. 6:24)

Who or what is your god? Is it God, the Father of our Holy Savior Jesus Christ, who sent forth the Holy Spirit? Or, do you possess some other god...a false god...like your own acquisition of greater wealth, fame, power and influence, social status, political influence or any other false gods? Is your source of Truth now Google, Microsoft, Amazon, Comcast, any government body or maybe some Wall Street tycoon and his or her financial tools and toys? Where are you in this one lifetime? Does God matter at all to you and HOW you freely choose to live out each and every hour of your days?

Does God really matter to you? Only YOU can truthfully answer this profound question in a full and brutally honest manner. No one else can answer this question for you. I remind you, others and myself that God extends to you and all people this gift of life. What might you have done to merit this undeserved gift? Anything at all? Who or what is your god? Reality and history confirm the existence of false gods. This is most apparent in more developed societies where food, clothing and shelter are no longer the major and most important priorities.

Our own society has grown quite complacent, even indifferent to the very real, serious and growing poverty across our nation, even here in our local communities, and sadly around the globe. Still, we remind ourselves that we need not worry about someone else's problems because they are not MY OWN problems. Why should I care about a lazy man or woman, or the fool who drinks and gets drunk, or uses drugs? These are NOT my problems. They are NOT my concern, and I am not responsible for those foolish enough to get drunk or high.

You might think, "Too bad for them." They are not my concern. Do these sound like words that might go through your mind, heart or spirit? I hope not! But maybe they do permeate your daily life. If so, then pray and ask yourself, What would Christ do? Who speaks to you, and through you? Is it our one true Father and Creator, our Lord and Savior Jesus Christ, the wisdom of the Holy Spirit? Or do you have some other god or gods?

Listen and hear our dear Lord. He speaks to you and through you. The prophet Amos (8:4) writes, "Hear this, you who trample upon the needy and destroy the poor of the land." Never will our dear Lord forget what we have done. Moses reminds us that we are not to worship false gods.

May we as gifts of God be attentive to the Gospel message. May we always seek to see, recognize and acknowledge that every human life is sacred, precious and holy. Every person possesses a God-created innate dignity and goodness. Things will always be mere things. Mammon, wealth, power and fame are all fleeting. In contrast, life in Christ is eternal. The choices are yours. Who is your false god, or is it our One True God?

September 22, 2019

TEMPORARY TOYS OR ETERNAL JOYS

He said, "Oh no, father Abraham, but if someone from the dead goes to them, they will repent." Then Abraham said, "If they will not listen to Moses and the prophets, neither will they be persuaded if someone should rise from the dead." (Luke 16:30–31)

Today throughout most, if not all nations, we find societies deeply believing in the old phrase, "Greed is good!" Wow! Millions of Americans are disenfranchised from the so-called greater wealth and concentration of power here in our society. In the ancient days, and far more than simply once, the ancient Jewish people turned toward wealth and away from God. This was made most clear when the Jews built the Golden Calf! Gold! Gold! Gold!

Apparently, they and all too many of our modern citizens subscribe to that old "Golden Rule": He who has the gold rules. I beg to differ with such a false assumption. But this is now the well-established and widely accepted foundational principle to which our modern society subscribes.

Wealth, fame and fortune are all fleeting! They come and they go! They can help destroy a just society by chipping away at the so called "common good," which must be the cornerstone of any fair, just and democratic society. However, the Gospel of Jesus time and again reminds us that we as individuals and as a society should seek to live out the Gospel by putting our faith into action. Our own lives are pure unearned God-given gifts. Our Lord will never judge a person based on their asset–liability ratio. Never! This is simply a man-made way of establishing who might be considered to be more successful than some other person. It's all a game. In the end, rich or poor, we will die, and in dying we will take none of our acquired toys with us. Like the poor homeless man who dies, the well-connected, rich and powerful will be laid to rest. Five or ten years from that burial day, society will go on not knowing anything about that rich or powerful person. Rather, society will always be indifferent toward that so-called successful person. Time continues to march on!

Today, we as a Church are at a crossroads in our institutional decisions as to the modern American Church. Cardinals and bishops, priests, deacons, monks and religious sisters and brothers, all of us MUST rely on the Catholic laity to help us rebuild our national Church, the faith of our modern Catholics and the quality of a Catholic education for our younger Catholics. You can place your lifelong efforts and goals in the almighty greenback. Or, in part, you can use your own time, talents and treasures and stoop down, in a life spent helping to strengthen, renew and build up the Church, and thus the Kingdom of God here at hand. This is simultaneously a Divine invitation and a real challenge. What is your lifetime really about? Have you time to give to the Church, the Body of Christ, and the people of God? I think you do. I think, if you are brutally honest with yourself, you too will humbly realize just how blessed you are, and that there is much work to be done in our Lord's vineyard. Come closer to our Lord. Live out the Gospel. God grants you life. What do you give back to our dear Lord? How do you put your faith into action?

September 29, 2019

DISCIPLES ANOINTED TO SERVE

"When you have done all you have been commanded, say, 'We are unprofitable servants; we have done what we were obliged to do'" (Luke 17:10). These ancient Scripture words echo today. By your Catholic Baptism, you were welcomed into the Church, as a child of God, a modern disciple of Christ, a member of the larger Body of Christ. Hopefully, through either a Catholic education, CCD or both, as well as family teachings and traditions, you have been able to first witness and then actually realize the Divine relationship with you personally, but also with the broader society, and the world at large. God is for you! Who could be against you? Are you with our good Lord?

In today's larger society and even within our modern Church, there is much desire to outdo the other guy, to accumulate greater power, fame or fortune. We want to be "NUMERO UNO" or number one! We want to shine as some great success in our family, local community or out in the broader society. None of these desires, hopes or goals have anything to do with the Gospel message. Nothing at all!

Your own life is already a sacred, precious and holy life. It is precisely because God has created you out of Divine love and in His image and likeness. What are you going to do to accept this infinite Divine love, Divine justice and Divine mercy? What are you doing today? Our Lord has a place for you in the unfolding of His kingdom here at hand. Are you being attentive to our Lord? Do you pray each day? Do you read Holy Scripture? Do you receive the Holy Sacraments on a regular basis? Our Lord created your life and continues to breathe life into you. Our Lord waits for you, and all prodigal sons and daughters to come home. Our Lord waits for you, me and also those searching for greater truth.

Pray every day. Then pray more. In doing so, through the combination of prayers, acts of compassion, daily prayers and a deep awareness of God's presence in your daily life, you can mature in your spiritual relationship with the Divine. In a spirit of love, be attentive to the Gospel. Be humbled to be invited to go out into the world and proclaim the Gospel with both words and actions. At the end of each day, be humbled by the worthiness of your own life, the God-given, and innate dignity God has granted you, and of course, the many abilities and gifts with which God has blessed you. Then, in a spirit of thanksgiving, be humbled and be at peace.

October 6, 2019

THE THANKFUL LEPER

In the times of Christ, any child, woman or man inflicted with leprosy was rejected by their own family, neighbors and certainly strangers. They were thought to have been inflicted with leprosy as a result of their forebears' or their own evil. Leprosy, like other serious health conditions, was seen as being an act of evil, and the people suffering from it and other horrendous health conditions were rejected by all and looked down on by their peers and society at large. This kind of treatment of people, human beings, we might find difficult to imagine. Nonetheless that was the society in the times of Christ and His apostles and disciples.

In addition, the one leper who came back to thank Jesus was a Samaritan. Jews and Samaritans despised, even hated, one another. They did so because the Samaritans were seen as being an ancient tribe that was unfaithful to Judaism. For a Samaritan leper to return to Jesus, a Jew, and be thankful to Jesus, a faithful Jew, was almost unimaginable. Even then, tribalism was a cause of serious social prejudices shared by even the mainstream society.

This leper who returned to thank Jesus offered to follow in Christ's company. This rejected, disabled Samaritan man, a rejected stranger, offered to walk humbly in the company of the mostly Jewish disciples of Christ. Our Father sent fourth his only begotten son, our savior Jesus Christ. He came to teach and preach, to heal and forgive, to reconcile humanity with the divine. Our savior Jesus Christ died and rose in fulfillment of the ancient prophets, for ALL of God's peoples.

The salvation Christ obtained for all humanity was a purely unearned gift granted by God, our Father, via Christ, His only begotten Son. Christ paid the eternal price for eternal salvation for all the generations who preceded His time on earth. He also paid the ultimate price for ALL his contemporaries. Last, Christ died and rose in fulfillment for ALL generations to follow His time here among humanity. The Samaritan leper understood this. He gave great heartfelt thanks. He asked our Lord, "Lord, what can I do for You?" Christ's answer to that ancient leper echoes in your own heart, mind and spirit. Our dear Lord, Jesus Christ, invites you, me and all humanity, to come closer, to be healed of whatever ails us and to walk humbly in the company of Christ. Our Lord invites us, and what is your answer to this unearned spiritual invitation from our Holy Savior? Pray and pray more. Follow in Christ's company. Be humbled by His infinite love. Then be still and quiet, and in that stillness, find peace. Last, pray in a spirit of heartfelt gratitude.

October 13, 2019

PRAY FOR PRIESTS

Today I write this column asking you to cut out my Prayer for Priests *and place it in your prayer book, Bible, with your rosary, on the refrigerator, in your car or another place you will see it. Then when you see it, be willing to take a few moments each day and pray for priests. As a parish priest, I can personally attest to the challenges, distrust and doubts people sometimes hold against today's Catholic priests. It really is a sad reality! But, it is the real world today! I pray for myself and all priests, but especially for the young priests. They face these and certainly unknown challenges. I pray for our younger priests (in their forties and younger), that they will be brutally frank and honest with themselves, their fellow priests, bishops and all religious priests, brothers and sisters. Today's extremely secular society fosters, even encourages, people to see our Roman Catholic faith as being nothing but "a nice story about some ancient teacher named Jesus." Please make time every day and pray. You are but one person. But, together, as we pray on a daily basis, we become an "Army of Prayers." We lift up our prayers, our cries and our dreams to our beloved Lord. And we trust, believe and go forward, knowing with heartfelt certitude that our dear Lord is with us and will enable our frail and broken priests to stoop down and one stone at a time begin and ultimately complete the rebuilding of our American Catholic Church. We need the vocations for priesthood, religious lives of sisters and brothers, and more permanent deacons. Let us pray. Today I ask you to please pray for priests. Thank you. Peace and many blessings.*

—Fr. Michael Briese

Prayer for Priests

Our Father in heaven, we pray You will continue to watch over, guide and protect our priests and bishops. We ask You, dear Lord, to hear their prayers, the cries of their heart and their heart-felt desire to more fully grasp Your hands. You are our Good Shepherd. You, Lord, humbly walk in the company of Your priests. We give thanks to You, and we ask You, O Lord, to awaken our lives and bless us with greater faith, greater hope and greater love. We plead You will always protect us from the snares of the wicked, temptations from fools, and the countless sins of which we are quite capable. Lord, we give You praise for Your love, mercy, forgiveness and countless blessings. You, Lord, are our true Creator. All Glory and Honor is Yours as we give thanks and praise to You, dear Lord. Dearly beloved Father, Savior and Holy Spirit, in humble gratitude and deep awe, we give thanks to You for our holy priesthood. We give praise to You who live and reign forever and ever. AMEN.

October 20, 2019

GOD'S MERCY

Your life is a holy life, a sacred life and a precious life. It is precisely because God created you, man and all humanity out of Divine love and in His image and likeness. God has a role for you to play in the unfolding of his kingdom at hand. Our Lord sees in you, and in all people, the beauty resting within each and every person. Are you a righteous disciple of Christ? Are you a mere human being, a person whose own self bears its own shortcomings, imperfections and brokenness? Every person carries innate goodness and our one common imperfect humanity.

I suggest we humbly acknowledge our one common imperfect human nature. In doing so, we can recognize our shared dignity as members of the human race. This is easier to discuss than to actually live out.

Fidelity to Christ both invites and encourages us to recognize the goodness of our Lord in all peoples. If we pray to ask our dear Lord to guide us throughout the passing of each day, and we are willing to imitate Christ, it will become easier and more natural for us to live our lives with respect, compassion and love for our fellow human beings. The Gospel message is a road map to HOW and WHY our Lord invites us as imperfect human beings to enter more fully into His company.

We can be both righteous and sinful people. We are at once living our lives with many contradictions. The signs of God are all around us. But if we do not look, we will not see. If we do not listen, we will not hear. We are both righteous and sinners. May we be humbled by our one common humanity. And may we be willing to imitate Christ. AMEN.

October 27, 2019

RICH MAN'S POVERTY OF HEART

Zacchaeus was a well-to-do and an influential tax collector. Many in his locality disliked him. Others even despised him. His greatest sin was his obvious greed. Greed is one of the ancient seven deadly sins because greed can and will in the long-term oppress, deny and even destroy one's neighbors, family members and community, even in faraway places. Greed was rejected by the ancient Jews and their blessed prophets. Whenever greed has been allowed to flourish, establish itself and be accepted, it has always wrought destruction to the broader communities, whole peoples and even nations. Zacchaeus understood this and fully grasped the self-realization that his own success was directly and deeply rooted in the established and organized and legally permissible oppression of other people. Even a simple old man and woman understood what was going on in those ancient days.

Economic oppression, unjust taxation, centralized political powers and influence concentrated among the few, forced common people into a society in which common, good, hard-working and honest people were easily kept powerless. Back then, economic oppression dictated society. Concentration of wealth in our modern society isn't much different. However, the principle of greed and its widespread acceptance among our modern people of wealth, power and influence continues to exert and concentrate our democratic principles and powers within the hands of a small number of institutions, agencies, international corporations, particular fields of very powerful political lobbies and among the top one percent of American citizens. Such a concentration of power and wealth has not been present in America since the early 1920s.

In our own communities we still must confront such concentrated social, economic and political oppression. Zacchaeus was to Jesus who our local wealthy powerhouses and citizens would be to Christ today. Will our local Roman Catholics, Protestants, Jews and those of other great faiths come together and join with one another in ways that will help to build up, renew and strengthen our one common humanity and the dignity that is granted unto every human being by God? Will these blessed ones of great faith reach out to engage, accept and assist the least among us? Will those already blessed in countless ways join together and fight against growing local hunger, homelessness and the growing need for adequate seasonal clothing? We can and we should.

Zacchaeus through Christ was transformed and put his faith into action. His exemplary faith and trust in Christ provides a brightly shining example of just how one human being can transform the lives of others, especially those counted among the less fortunate. Will we ever draw near to our Lord and Savior? Do we adore and pursue some other god? Do we imitate Christ? Zacchaeus shows us a road to follow. AMEN.

November 3, 2019

GOD OF THE LIVING

    Moses called out, "Lord, the God of Abraham, the God of Isaac, and the God of Jacob; and he is not God of the dead, but of the living, for to him all are alive" (Luke 20:38). Our ancient Roman Catholic faith sustains this ancient understanding that our God has since the beginning of human history been the God whose infinite and immeasurable Divine love was exemplified at that first holy moment when God breathed a lifetime into Adam and then Eve…all men and women. God's immense love always has been, is now and forever shall be freely granted unto humanity. Why? Solely because God, the Creator of humanity, wills that His Love shall always exist, prevail and exemplify His own invitation to all past generations, today's generations and the generations to come.

    God's Divine mercy, Divine justice and Divine love can, at best, be imitated by you, me and all humanity. Though every person, regardless of their station in life, can only seek to imitate the God of Moses, Isaac and Jacob. We cannot be the same as God. However, God sustains human history precisely because our Divine Lover asks you, me and every human being to imitate His Divine love. You can do this, as can I, and every human being. The choices to do so are choices we, God's people, will make. Simply ask, who is your god this day and throughout your past and passing daily life? Is your god, our one true and full God, our Creator the true Divine, the One who rests within the very depth of your being? Or, have you made room for some man-made god? To whom is your heart a shelter? The God of Moses or some sort of other, more modern god?

Only you can truthfully and more fully answer these questions. But, you owe yourself the truth! And you get today and maybe tomorrow, or a long future to ask, address and truthfully and honestly answer this profound question. Our beloved Creator invites you, me and all His peoples to come closer, draw near and spend some time in His company. There you can more fully discover, grasp and grow into a faith-filled modern disciple of Christ;

a person whose heart is afire with the love only God can give. Your open heart, mind and spirit will enable you to more fully realize and love He Who Is and Always Will Be. Learn from the ancients such as Moses, Isaac and Jacob. Learn from the holy apostles, Mary, the countless early martyrs and even from your own elders or others whose lives exemplified their strong faith. Our dear Lord and Savior cries out to you. Hear our beloved Lord's Divine invitation and answer Him. May our good Lord bless you now and forever. AMEN.

November 10, 2019

PERSEVERANCE

"You will be hated by all because of my name, but not a hair on your head will be destroyed. By your perseverance you will secure your lives" (Luke 21:17–18) Awaken every breaking dawn keenly aware our good and gracious Lord is at your side, in your company and willing to walk humbly in your midst. Be taken aback by the Divine mercy our Lord bestows on you, within you, and expressed unto others by you. Yes, indeed! Our Lord is with us now and until the hour of our death.

No person will ever live their entire lifetime without seeing and or experiencing others' outright lies, cold indifference, hatred, betrayal or malice. It is all part of humanity's one common thread—our one common and imperfect human nature. Be prepared for those times in your life. All too often the most severe injuries thrust on a person are not caused by some total stranger. No! More often than not, such malice and painful events occur precisely because a family member, close friend or entrusted associate turns on you, betrays you and forces you to come face-to-face with a very painful moment or event in your life. It can sear or seriously burn into one's heart, mind or spirit a pain or injury that is deep and severe. That kind of betrayal and deep wound will not be cured by your own return of such ugly and malicious words or actions. Not at all!

Instead, our betrayed and crucified Lord reminds us that we are to forgive those who trespass against us. St. Francis of Assisi makes the most sense in these relationships as he wrote the following words:

Lord, make me an instrument of your peace: Where there is hatred, let me sow charity; Where there is injury, pardon; Where there is error, the truth; Where there is doubt, the faith; Where there is despair...hope; Where there is darkness, light; and Where there is sadness...joy.. O Divine Master, Grant that I may not so much seek to be consoled, as to console.

To be understood as to understand; To be loved as to love. For it is in giving that we receive; It is in pardoning that we are pardoned; And it is in dying to ourselves that we are born to eternal life.

This is a simple, yet powerful prayer…a road map of HOW to journey throughout this one God-given lifetime. It is a way to run the race, go the extra mile, and to do so in the company of Christ. In this, your one lifetime, the choices are yours to make. Strive to live this one lifetime in the company of Christ. And may all people be humbled to journey throughout this one lifetime in the company of Christ. AMEN.

November 17, 2019

THE GOOD CRIMINAL

Then he said, "Jesus, remember me when you come into your kingdom." He replied to him, "Amen, I say to you, today you will be with me in Paradise." (Luke 23: 42–43)

You and I, all human beings, are much like this criminal. Our dearly beloved Creator grants us this one lifetime and does so without attaching any terms or conditions. Our Father gifts us with our sacred, precious and holy human life. He grants us every minute of every hour of every day, and every passing week, month, year, decade and ongoing time itself. God clearly showed humanity, and all who were willing to look and see, to listen and hear, and to more fully understand that our creator had sent forth His only begotten Son, His Holy Child to walk among us. And Jesus walked and entered into some very holy moments and hours as He unconditionally loved others, even His enemies; He preached not simply by words but by His daily and holy life; He taught not merely with words or lectures but by the way He lived out the Gospel in both words and works. And Christ taught when He gathered together with His twelve apostles at a dinner table. There He broke the bread, gave it to His apostles and said, "Take this all of you and eat of it, for this is my Body which will be given up for you. Do this in memory of me." Then He took the cup and said, "Take this all of you and drink from it for this is the Cup of my Blood, the new and everlasting covenant. It will be shed for you and for all. Do this in memory of me." This holy meal, historically known as the Last Supper will forever exemplify God's infinite love, Divine mercy and the Holy Name of Jesus.

The "good criminal" next to Christ clearly recognized God's infinite love, Divine mercy and the fulfillment of the ancient prophets as he saw, spoke with, and came to fully grasp that the promised Savior was right there and was being treated as a common criminal, a man fully exposed to public rejection, ridicule and condemnation. God gives and gives unto you, me and the whole world. God does so every single passing minute of human history. When will we ever learn to see, accept and humbly give much thanks to our one common Creator?

God, our Creator, sends Jesus, the expected Christ and the King of Kings. He was to be executed between two thieves. Jesus promises salvation to one of the two criminals. This criminal was the first to be assured eternal life by Jesus our Savior. He was a criminal! Jesus did not first say this to St. Peter, Mother Mary or any other apostles. Rather, Jesus welcomed a dying criminal whose heart was renewed as he freely sought to believe in Christ and to live his life in the company of Christ. Now that is a pure and holy life. Can you, I or anyone TRUTHFULLY say, "I have surrendered my own ways," unto our dear Lord? And do I live my life in the ways of Christ? Think about this. Pray about this. Then, let us give thanks to our dear Lord. AMEN.

November 24, 2019

A WINTER COAT

He was a happy young man. He needed a winter coat but without a steady job he had almost no money, very little food and no steady place to lay his head. He was living in the local woods. At night the temperatures would go down into the mid or high thirties. He had just received a winter coat from a stranger, an older lady whom he had met over at a local liquor store. She gave him five dollars and he used the money to buy a small lunch. He was quite grateful for her kindness because her five dollars enabled him to enjoy a modest lunch. Now he found himself with very little money, little food and without steady housing. What was he to do?

Late that afternoon he was inside his small tent in the woods. Suddenly there was a yell, a cry, a scream. He went outside and could see a young man about twenty-four years old. He walked over to this stranger and asked him, "Why are you screaming and yelling?" The young man responded, "I am the Lord, your God. I am a stranger in need. You see me, but do not believe me. Your doubts and fears prevail throughout your current daily life. You have faith. Now use it. I am the Lord, your God. Blessed is he who walks in my company. Do you hear what I hear? Do you see what your eyes see, or is your heartfelt sight impaired? Where is your heart? Is there deep faith, hope and love inside your heart? Come closer to me and find gratitude, awe and greater faith, hope and love."

When the young poor man heard all this, he was both shocked and pleasantly surprised to meet our Lord. He turned around because he had heard some noise. Coming toward him was another slightly older man, about twenty-nine years old. Though they were total strangers, they both met and freely acknowledged one another, introduced themselves to one another and were quite accepting in their brief conversation. The man with the winter coat quickly saw that this slightly older gentleman had no winter coat. So, the younger man took off his own winter coat and handed it over to the older homeless man.

What had just happened? The poor among the poor met, and one of these two poor men quickly saw and recognized that the older gentleman had no winter coat. He had no money. He had nothing. He had no paycheck or salary coming to him. Like the younger man, this older man was also a mere poor man. He had nothing—exactly what he had when he came into this world. But he had a life, every breath he had and would ever take, his joys to be alive and a spirit of trust in the Lord. Though poor in materials, this older poor man already knew that his greatest gift was his love for his fellow human beings. Now, a younger man freely chose to take off his only winter coat and gave it away to his older brother in Christ.

The younger man had just given away his most valuable gift to a peasant who entered into his own impoverished life. Be attentive, stay awake and alert, and humbly acknowledge those times in your life when Christ briefly entered into your daily life. He comes most often in the form of a poor and simple person. Amid the poor you will find your greatest gift: the Christ Child. AMEN.

November 28, 2019

GOD AND NATIONS

He shall judge between the nations, and set terms for many peoples. They shall beat their swords into plowshares and their spears into pruning hooks; One nation shall not raise the sword against another, nor shall they train for war again. House of Jacob, come, let us walk in the light of the Lord. (Isa. 2:4–5)

Today in early 21st century, humanity continues, in its refusal to listen and live by these ancient sacred words found in Isaiah 2:1–5. Imagine, even ancient peoples understood the great destruction wars produce. Human beings become carnage. They are considered to be mere things. War is more often than not rooted in deeply seeded hatred. Today's ongoing ISIS wars and battles confirm all this. American, British and French, other allied soldiers, and military forces have killed over one hundred thousand men, women and children in our last twenty years of fighting selective wars. Our government leaders spout the right kinds of words, apologizing for the so-called accidental deaths of innocent people. But words are cheap expressions of hot air. Our leaders know this. So do the new widows, widowers and parents. Isaiah knew this. Why do we almost always favor war and killing over peace and follow up efforts fostering peace through education, addressing poverty, hunger, adequate jobs and the encouragement of families over continuous division and ongoing hatred?

Isaiah knew thousands of years ago that war is almost always a bad, even evil option and rarely moral or justifiable. In our more recent history, World War II was absolutely a necessary war and morally justifiable in our ancient Roman Catholic Tradition. No war after World War II and prior to our aggressive defensive attack in Afghanistan was a moral war in the Roman Catholic Tradition. They were wars pursued because of a few who were in power. Under American constitutional law, no president is to declare war without the informed advice and consent and majority support of the

US Congress. The first President George Bush did this because he fully knew and respected the constitutional laws of our nation. He respected the laws of our land. No other president has done that since.

Isaiah understood the hatred and oppression that can grow in men's hearts and mankind's willingness to hate, kill, destroy and even eradicate other peoples and their nations. Such leadership is morally repugnant, reprehensible and immoral. Today over 30,000 common Americans...men and women...have come home from wars without their minds, vision and all their limbs. They continue to suffer immensely, too many have lost their dignity, their human spirit, their marriages and families, and these true heroes still suffer daily. They are prisoners of rich and powerful men and women who have enjoyed their own increased wealth, fame and power. This is a modern version of just WHY the ancient prophet Isaiah wrote these ancient words. When will we heed this God-given wisdom? When? Let us pray for peace.

December 1, 2019

EXPECTATION

Now the people were filled with expectation, and all were asking in their hearts whether John might be the Messiah. John answered them all, saying, "I am baptizing you with water, but one mightier than I is coming. I am not worthy to loosen the thongs of his sandals." (Luke 3:15–16)

The only plans I have are the plans I have not made as I wait in expectation and listen with an attentive heart and actively pursue my lifelong intention to go forth with God. Lord, You journey in my company. My days are numbered. You bless me with life, the breaking of every dawn, time itself, every breath I take, the countless beauties discovered throughout creation and most important…Your provision of Your Spirit that rests within me.

O God, my God, You walk in my company and are always willing to provide the Light of the World in the midst of my human brokenness. Lord, Your tender words, infinite love and immense compassion bring healing, change and renewal to my own human imperfection.

O Lord, I ask, "Who am I to make plans for my life as I live each day with a sweet awareness of Your eternal presence? Each hour of each day is Your time, dear Lord. Who am I to fully grasp and understand Your very presence? Who am I to determine just WHAT You have in store for me this very day?"

Lord, I abandon my own wants and plans and instead I wait… I wait for You O Lord to gather and find rest and stillness within the very depth of my heart, and to make clear what You ask of me this hour, this day. And so I wait… Come dear Lord, gather within the very depths of my heart. Lord, make clear what You ask of me this very day.

O God, my God, You sent Your only beloved Son to invite Your people to draw near. Your Holy Spirit echoes this ancient Divine invitation within the very depths of countless broken lives. Lord, slow us down. Rather, teach us to read Holy Scripture, to pray and nourish the wisdom of our heart, to seek Your justice and good counsel, and to listen carefully to others. O Lord, teach me Your ways, encourage me to persevere as I learn about our faith, and HOW to live out Your Holy Gospel as I strive to put my faith into action.

Lord, I pray, and humanity prays, that You will grant all peoples and nations Your peace. You make time to walk in my company and for this lifelong blessing of Divine mercy I give thanks to You, my dear Lord. Blessed are You, O Lord, our God. Holy is Your Name.

O Lord, I wait in expectation and am keenly aware that my life is truly Your life. O Lord, in the end there are three great gifts: faith, hope and love—and the greatest of these is love. Lord, take my one life and make me a true and greater gift of Your love. My dear Lord, I offer You this prayer in a spirit of awe, humility and thanksgiving.

December 16, 2019

BEHOLD THE LAMB OF GOD

In the Roman Catholic tradition, we see Jesus Christ as being the expected Savior of the world. We see Him as the One sent forth by His Father in fulfillment of the ancient prophets. We see Jesus as being the Son of Mary, the Holy Virgin and Joseph the blessed father. We see Christ as being the Lamb of God who takes away the sins of the world. Still, to this very day, and this actual moment, we see Jesus as being the Divine One whose presence has already transformed billions of lives, powerful empires and even countless human hearts, minds spirits and daily lives.

By coming into the midst of mere human beings, the Prince of Peace set the example for all of us to imitate. In our modern society, we are bombarded daily with all kinds of messages as to WHY you need this product or service.

You will have a better life, if only you… We see pictures of so-called "cool" products or places and we receive tons and tons of reasons as to WHY you MUST have this or go there. We get bombarded with words, ads, images, or a combination of these and other modes of advertising and marketing tools. Wow!

When you have lived through all of one day, ask yourself this question, Today, HOW MANY minutes and/or hours did I listen to advertising? Well, God sent forth His only begotten Son, our Savior Jesus Christ, so that YOU can have the time and place needed to encounter Christ. Yesterday, how many hours did you see or listen to or experience advertising or marketing? And, how many hours did you give to Christ? Think about this. Are you alive simply to consume goods or services? Did you know that YOU are alive because God has created you out of Divine love and in His image and likeness, and He has a role for YOU to play in the unfolding of His kingdom here at hand? Spend some time with our dear Lord. Seek to encounter our beloved Lord in silence. Encounter our dear Lord, when you hand maybe a five dollar bill to a homeless woman. Or, see the presence of

Christ when you visit a frail elderly relative. And, encounter Christ when a simple and innocent child looks up at the setting sun and tells you ever so simply that "the setting sun looks like God's balloon." Listen and our dearest Lord will enter more fully into your heart, mind and spirit.

You already are a part of the Body of Christ. Be present to our Lord. Allow our Lord to guide you. Your daily awareness and encounter with our Lord will always enable you to get through any dark times. Be prayerful and thankful. Be awed and pray daily. Last, humbly acknowledge our Lord's anchor in your heart, mind and spirit. Be humbled as you stand in God's presence. For indeed the Lord is with you now, and until the hour of your death. As it is written, we will go "from dust to dust and ashes to ashes." And eternal life shall be ours for the asking. May our loving Creator invite you to come closer, and in His company to find rest and stillness. AMEN.

January 19, 2020

LOVE AS PURE GIFT

Our dear Lord and Savior Jesus Christ calls you, me and every member of our one human race to love. Sounds easy? It's not! Still, the Gospels are clear, declarative and resolute in their invitation to draw near to our Lord, to live life in ways that build up, rather than destroy. You and all people are called by Christ to make choices to love. We are reminded by St. Paul that there are many ways, even countless ways, to love. In his Letter to Romans it is written, "If ministry, in ministering; if one is a teacher, in teaching; if one exhorts, in exhortation; if one contributes, in generosity; if one is over others, with diligence; if one does acts of mercy, with cheerfulness." (Romans 12:7-8). Love begets love.

Love reflects goodness. Goodness reflects God. God is goodness. Can you, I and other people, right here in our own families, our local communities and all around us, try and persevere at living our one holy, sacred and precious life in accord with the exemplary life of Christ? Yes, we can. It is written, "Let us not grow tired of doing good, for in due time we shall reap our harvest, if we do not give up" (Gal. 6:9). Every single human being walking our planet has a role to play in the unfolding of God's kingdom here at hand. What is your role in this Divine plan? How will you discern and strive to live out your life as it unfolds one hour, one day at a time? What does God ask from you this very hour, this very day? The only way to discern the answers to these and other questions is through prayer. Be encouraged to start or develop, or share your own prayer life and daily prayerful activities. We can all learn from one another. No one will ever possess the entire answer to the previous questions. But, together, as modern disciples of Christ, as a community of modern believers, and as truly Christ-centered children of God, we can lift up this world and in particular our small corner in this much larger world.

Are you in search of our good Lord? Are you seeking greater faith, greater hope, and greater love? Are you in your faith aware that our dear Lord asks you, this very hour, to go out among our brothers and sisters, even those who are strangers to us? Also, our Lord asks us to bring His Good News and greater faith, greater hope and greater love into their lives. Doing this will require a price! One might say doing this, can demand or extract a burdensome toll, even true pain and suffering. Still, like the Suffering Servant, we freely recognize, welcome and strive to live out our lives, not in "my own ways," but rather in the ways of Jesus Christ. He has been, is now and always will be the Way, the Truth and the Light!

Is your heart attentive to this Divine invitation? How will you respond to our dear Lord's kind invitation? If you choose NOT to answer this Divine invitation, Time over many years will answer this Divine invitation for you! It is your faith, your choice, and your decision. Will you freely choose to walk humbly in the company of Christ? May we always remember what the ancient prophet Micah wrote, "You have been told, O mortal, what is good, and what the Lord requires of you: Only to do justice and to love goodness, and to walk humbly with your God" (Mic. 6:8). AMEN.

January 26, 2020

PRESENTATION OF THE LORD

The child's father and mother were amazed at what was said about him; and Simeon blessed them and said to Mary his mother, "Behold, this child is destined for the fall and rise of many in Israel, and to be a sign that will be contradicted (and you yourself a sword will pierce) so that the thoughts of many hearts may be revealed." (Luke 2:33–35)

One prayer written to celebrate this great Feast Day of the Presentation of the Lord is written, "Almighty ever-living God, we humbly implore your majesty that, just as your Only Begotten Son was presented on this day in the Temple in the substance of our flesh, so, by your grace, we may be presented to you with minds made pure." Do you come before our dear Lord with purity of mind, heart and spirit? Are you a blessed person whose heart is attuned to Jesus Christ and attentive to His Holy Word? Is your daily life, a life deeply rooted in the Gospel? Is your mind alert, keenly aware and willing to humbly acknowledge the Almighty presence our Lord plays in the unfolding of your only one sacred, precious and holy life? Where is our Lord, the Holy Child in your life today, in this holy hour, and at this one particular God-created moment? Pray these holy words,

"May the Spirit of our Lord come upon me. May the holy wisdom of His Holy Spirit permeate my heart, mind and spirit. May His Holy Spirit grasp my hands and take me, guide me, and create in me a humble heart and a spirit on fire with our dear beloved Lord's infinite love, mercy and justice. Hear O Lord, the cries of my heart! Stir me, guide me, and mold me into the devout person you ask me to be and become. AMEN."

Prayer is the language of the human heart. Cry out, "Speak Lord and answer me." Then humbly give thanks unto the very One who breathed life into you at that sacred, precious and holy moment of your conception. At that moment, in the unfolding of human history, our dear Lord welcomed you into his ever-expanding universe. Like the Presentation of the Lord, you were born, and at birth you experienced your own Presentation of a holy innocent child who first was presented to family, and then unto all humanity, as being, and becoming yet another blessed gift bestowed upon humanity. At that moment you experienced your own holy moment when life triumphed and goodness prevailed. And in that one holy moment, our beloved Creator saw you, smiled upon you, and recognized that in your creation He was quite pleased. What a great gift you have been, are now and hopefully shall be forever. AMEN.

February 2, 2020

SURPASSING RIGHTEOUSNESS

We quickly are approaching the great season of Lent—a season of forty days when we prepare ourselves for the upcoming Passion of our dear Lord and Savior Jesus Christ. Let us NOT mistake Lent as just some liturgical season of the liturgical year. No, the message of Lent, the purpose of God's only begotten Son being sent forth to teach and preach, to heal and raise from the dead is far more complex! Lent is a spiritual moment during which our ongoing and passing lifetimes during which we, as practicing Catholics and Christians, are willing to slow down, pray more and strive to improve our own willingness and abilities to follow in the footsteps of Christ.

Wake up! Stay alert! Our Lord is with us, now and until the hour of our holy death. Awaken! Awaken! Stay alert! He is among us!

He is here! Seek and you will find! Knock and the door shall be opened! Ask and it shall be given! Are you a person who really does pray? I sure hope so! If not, it's sort of like walking—once you try it and fall down time and again, after a while, you will get it (prayer) down pat. But spiritually you have to be willing to work at it, fail and fail again and then only slowly over many years, you too, like the Apostles, shall be brought closer into the greater fullness of our Holy Lord's Divine presence. Do you hear this Divine invitation? If so, what is your response?

If you really want to draw closer to our beloved Lord, if you really want to improve your faith journey and if you truly wish to more fully embrace and imitate Christ, then, like Christ, you must be willing to empty yourself off your old self, as a person of this world, and enter more fully into a daily life centered on Christ, deeply embraced and lived out in conjunction with Christ's teachings and to become a modern disciple whose heart is on fire with greater faith, greater hope and greater love. Do this and you, too, shall come face-to-face with God!

Michael Briese

We are all called to NOT judge others. We should always be willing to "dare to care" about others. Can you accept this Divine dare? Do you have the willingness, abilities, concern or care? You will only ever find out when you decide to walk humbly and in the company of our dear Risen Lord! Always choose to avoid gossip, refuse to seek vengeance, hold no animosities toward other people, do not turn away from any person in need, pray for mercy for your own self and also for others, even strangers in need. Last, be humbled by our dear Lord's eternal love. Then say, "AMEN!"

February 16, 2020

WHEN YOU MEET THE POOR CHRIST

"For where your treasure is, there also will your heart be." (Matt. 6:21)

"'Come,' says my heart, 'seek his face'; your face, Lord, do I seek! Do not hide your face from me." (Ps. 27:8–9)

"At night I cry aloud in your presence. Let my prayer come before you." (Ps. 88:23)

"Relieve the troubles of my heart; bring me out of my distress. Look upon my affliction and suffering; take away all my sins." (Ps. 25:17–18)

"He will shelter you with his pinions, and under his wings you may take refuge." (Ps. 91:4)

"My dear child: grace, mercy, and peace from God the Father and Christ Jesus our Lord." (2 Tim. 1:2)

"They are your servants, your people, whom you freed by your great might and strong hand." (Neh. 1:10)

"Remember your compassion and your mercy, O Lord, for they are ages old…Do not let my enemies gloat over me…Redeem Israel, O God, from all our distress!" (Ps. 25:6, 2, 22)

"But I say to you, love your enemies, and pray for those who persecute you, that you may be children of your heavenly Father." (Matt. 5:44–45)

"We shall be like him, for we shall see him as he is." (1 John 3:2)

"Let us not grow tired of doing good, for in due time we will reap our harvest, if we do not give up." (Gal. 6:9)

"One does not live by bread alone, but by every word that comes forth from the mouth of God." (Matt. 4:4)

"Is it not sharing your bread with the hungry, bringing the afflicted and the homeless into your house; Clothing the naked when you see them, and not turning your back on your own flesh…if you lavish your food on the hungry and satisfy the afflicted; Then your light shall rise in the darkness, and your gloom shall become midday." (Isa. 58:7, 10)

"For I was hungry and you gave me food, I was thirsty and you gave me drink, a stranger and you welcomed me." (Matt. 25:35)

"Put on then, as God's chosen ones, holy and beloved, heartfelt compassion, kindness, humility, gentleness, and patience." (Col. 3:12)

"Whoever has two tunics should share with the person who has none. And whoever has food should do likewise." (Luke 3:11)

"Honor the Lord with your wealth, and with first fruits of all your produce; Then will your barns be filled with plenty, with new wine your vats will overflow." (Prov. 3:9–10)

"May the God of hope fill you with all joy and peace in believing, so that you may abound in hope by the power of the holy Spirit." (Rom. 15:13)

"Please let me see your glory!" (Exod. 33:18)

"'He will command his angels concerning you' and 'with their hands they will support you, lest you dash your foot against a stone.'" (Matt. 4:6)

"May we see better times! Lord, show us the light of your face!" (Ps. 4:7)

"If ministry, in ministering; if one is a teacher, in teaching; if one exhorts, in exhortation; if one contributes, in generosity; if one is over others, with diligence; if one does acts of mercy, with cheerfulness." (Rom. 12:7–8)

"But who am I, and who are my people, that we should have the means to contribute so freely? For everything is from You, and what we give is what we have from you." (1 Chron. 29:14)

"He will call upon me and I will answer; I will be with him in distress; I will deliver him and give him honor. With length of days I will satisfy him, and fill him with my saving power." (Ps. 91:15–16)

"For here we have no lasting city, but we seek the one that is to come...let us continually offer God a sacrifice of praise." (Heb. 13:14–15)

"In whose case the god of this age has blinded the minds of the unbelievers, so that they may not see the light of the gospel of the glory of Christ, who is the image of God." (2 Cor. 4:4)

"Into your hands I commend my spirit; you will redeem me, Lord, God of truth." (Ps. 31:6)

February 19, 2020

LOVE YOUR ENEMY

In our self-centered culture, it is NOT even logical to be concerned about another person. This world, or at least "my part" of the world is all about me, myself and I. Our society tells us to defame, ignore and even feel free to slander our family members, old friends, neighbors, fellow employees, public figures, clergy, educators, police and firemen. Society assures us that whatever we "feel," well, its "real" and "authentic" and should not be ignored. Who cares if one has an enemy? Like all those computer games, when you have an imagined or real "enemy" in life, then, just like in the game, you simply destroy that person, their reputation, their good name or even their livelihood or life. It is all about that old book title, *The Games People Play*. These words are a very accurate description of our current and ongoing society. But all those harsh words have absolutely nothing to do with the Gospel, Jesus Christ or even why you are here! Awaken! Stop placing your mind, heart and spirit under the controls of technology, high-tech machinery or that modern god of Google and its fellow corporate technology gods.

Why would you want to love your enemy? Glad you asked! When you prayerfully seek to love your enemy, you will, over the years, come to discover what true forgiveness is really about. Be or become a great forgiver! Truly, deep within the very depth of your being, develop the spiritual goodness needed to face the brutal reality, and once you can clearly see who your enemies are, then, at that very moment and on that same day, you go off by yourself. In silence, you close your eyes, cry whatever tears are required, and in sorrow, anger, bewilderment and a lack of any certainty, you simply pray and deeply believe that God will enable you to forgive those who trespassed against you—people who can legitimately be viewed as being your enemies—and YOU lift up your own fears, tears, uncertainty, disbelief and any doubts unto your dear Lord. You offer up your own humanity with all its imperfections and brokenness and offer your broken spirit, heart and mind unto our Lord on behalf of those who are your enemies.

WHY do this? Because it is what Christ did for you and me. Follow and live this one lifetime in the image and likeness of Christ.

Learn to love your enemy. Pray for your enemy. Forgive those who trespass against you. Never surrender your God-given heart, mind or soul unto another person, any corporation or government. You are here in this world precisely because God has a role for you to play in the unfolding of His kingdom here at hand. Ignore societal influences. Rather, pray throughout the passing of each hour and every day. Seek to live your life in a way that is Christ-centered. Be not afraid of the evil powers that lurk within the cold tombs of every person's heart. Rather, when you are forced to confront evil, pain, injuries, then respond to such harmful ways or words with love, mercy and forgiveness. I know it makes no sense! You are right! Just consider these words a Divine invitation unto you. Our Lord invites you to imitate His holy life, to pray more, to forgive others and sometimes your own self and even to love your enemy. Our Lord has spoken. How will you seek to live out our ancient faith?

February 23, 2020

HOW FORTUNATE
I AM

I try and I try each and every day. I work hard. I am honest. I am responsible. I respect other people. I do not cheat, lie or scam anyone. I look around and see many people whose cars are expensive, their clothes are too, and they seem to be talking about this most recent trip, or some trip from this past holiday season. They seem to make it in life, but compared to me, some of them do not impress me with having much respect toward other people. Some sound like they have a sense of superiority, or entitlement, or no need to work. I may be poor, but I have good ears.

I think about my dear Lord and all He grants unto me. I can work and so I always have food, clothing and shelter. I have always had a simple roof over my head, decent health and the determination to never quit or give up. I respect other people naturally because I treat others as I would wish to be treated. I have been blessed with a good family and loving friendships. My family and circle of friends like me, more often than not, are simple people, with modest means. We work hard. We are there for one another. Sure, we argue and shout, but at the end of the day, we are there for one another! I have and share such an abundance of blessings!

An old minister once told me that some people who enjoy real material success too often can be people who have no real personal depth. In short, their idea of success is their "score card" kept according to society's materialistic ideas of success. Yet, right there within them, they have little or no substance. Their daily lives are but one act following another act. Their life is at best superficial and is all about its superficial appearance. In short, they do not know who their "true self" really is. This makes sense. After all, if I do not pursue truth, if I do not dare to ask who I am and who I am meant to become, then just HOW can I really expect to find truth? The old minister told me, "I owe myself truth and to live my life being true to God." I think he was right.

Serving God By Serving Others

The world says one is fortunate based on their asset–liability ratio, their accumulation of toys such as, but not limited to, houses, stocks, cars and expensive suits. I have a roof over my head, food in the cupboard, clothes in my closet and some money to my name. For these great gifts I humbly give thanks to our dear beloved Father, His only begotten Son and the indwelling Holy Spirit. For this alone, I give my deep heartfelt thanks unto God all throughout each passing day. Do all people give thanks to God throughout the passing day? I would hope so! Without God, who am I? I cannot create even one ocean, let alone the birds of the air, the crops of the fields, the countless trees in the forests, the heavens above, the vast waterways of this world or its countless hills and mountains. God did all this. Why? I think God did all this and does so much more because His greatest gift to all of humanity remains His love. Without love what good is our world with its modern false gods and the modern godless desires to have more and more material things? His Son was raised as the son of a poor carpenter. This is a good reminder about how fortunate I am.

March 1, 2020

PRAYER FOR VICTORY OVER ILLNESS

Dearest Loving Lord,

Our hearts are infected with countless fears of death. A great and fearful silence now burdens too many hearts, minds and spirits. Death resulting from a seemingly unknown and untested illness has destroyed millions of lives around the world. This burdensome illness destroys far too many lives throughout Your modern world.

Lord, we ask You to enable the world's greatest researchers, innovators and men and women of great faith, greater hope, perseverance and tireless determination to use the greater knowledge already present here in our world to pursue, discover and develop the new pioneering knowledge needed to overcome this threatening worldwide epidemic. Lord, may death be no victor over life. May countless men and women never give up in their pioneering pursuit to defeat a somewhat mysterious cause of epidemic proportions! May humanity always prevail in its glorious everlasting pursuit to recognize, sustain, uphold and celebrate our one common human nature, the treasure contained within every human life, our innate human dignity and our God-given human goodness. We give thanks and are humbled by You, dear Lord, who so generously continues to speak to and through Your many holy peoples. O Lord, we thank You for the countless times when You have and always will lift up those who follow in Your footsteps.

May every man, woman and child come to discover that their own human life and every human life is already sacred, precious and holy precisely because God created all human life out of Divine love and in His image and likeness. Death is no victor over life. Even lost lives still hold a place in the unfolding of God's Kingdom here at hand.

Though confronted by a growing number of deaths and far too much suffering, may we never allow the devil's tool of fear to have dominion over our hearts, minds or spirits. May we use the God-created and God-granted gift of prayer as the instilled language of our own blessed and crying heart. There within the very depth of our own self we can discover and allow prayer to become now and forever the language of our own heart. May we pray throughout each passing hour and day. In prayer may we ask our dear Lord to grasp and rescue those who are suffering. May we allow silence to prevail there within the silence of one's prayerful heart. May we listen evermore closely as our dearly beloved Lord whispers within the very depth of one's very being. There in prayer and with a spirit of awe and humility may we ever more closely come face to face with God! Even when we experience illness and suffering, may we not permit the arrows that fly by day, or the evil spirits that can tempt us by night to prevail over God's many blessings. There within the very fiber of your being you will find God. Go there. Then be at peace with yourself, other people and our dear Lord.

Lord, give me the courage needed to acknowledge and persevere in my daily life even though I fully understand that suffering and human imperfections certainly can permeate the depth of one's own daily life. Lord, I ask, even beg You, to accept the prayerful offering of my own wounds and pains, and those that inflict my loved ones. Please, dear Lord, lift these burdens, this very precious cup from my shoulders. I offer them as gifts from my sacred but wounded heart. Please Lord, accept these cries from myself.

I have nothing more to bring as gifts to You, O Lord, my God. Lord, for far too long I have known You invite me to come closer and to pray from the very depths of my own being. Now, in pain, I beseech You, O Lord, my God. I beg You, teach me to pray with the simplicity of an innocent child and the wisdom of our elders. Lord, long ago I understood that since ancient days You have been, are now and forever shall be our one and only true God. There is no other. Hear, O Lord, the sounds of my cries as being heartfelt teardrops blessed with Your infinite love, Divine mercy and peace. Lord, You are our God and we are Your people.

Lord, we are begging You to heed the cries of the thousands now suffering from this dangerous and life-threatening virus. Hear, O Lord, the sounds of our countless heartfelt cries. Hear, dear Lord, and answer us as we lift up our prayers unto You our Almighty God. O Lord, send forth You Holy Spirit and Divine mercy and Divine justice. Lord, enable the world to recognize the Holy Name of our dear Lord and Savior Jesus Christ. In imitation of Christ, may we always strive to fight evil with greater faith, trust and love. We offer our prayers and the cries of our one collective prayerful human heart with greater faith, greater hope and greater love. Lord, we beg You to bless humanity with an abundance of healing, courage, greater faith, greater hope, greater love, spiritual consolation and steadfast renewal. AMEN.

March 13, 2020

BLESSINGS ON ME

Lord, You have always poured countless blessings onto humanity. For this alone, I give an abundance of thanks to You, O Lord, our God. My parents taught us to always say *please* and *thanks*. They taught us this so that one day as adults we would go out into society being adults whose own hearts and minds would be keenly aware that we so often are given or granted or provided a favor, a meal or hospitality that we did not earn or merit. These acts of kindness, generosity, and goodness were freely given by other people who asked for nothing in return. Our parents were smart! Somehow they understood that humanity could always use a little more goodness, thanksgiving and appreciation. They knew that decades ago and now decades later, we, their adult children, understand the profound value of this simple but invaluable understanding.

Lord, Your blessings on me are countless and have been throughout all my past days, and I believe will continue in abundance throughout my future days. Why? Because our dear Lord extended unto you, me and every human being a brief moment in His Eternal Story. This brief time is our one lifetime. It will be no shorter and no longer. I try in some insignificant way to realize this God-given gift of life on a daily basis. Each day I give my heartfelt thanks to our God and His Divine mercy, justice and love. We can at best only seek to more fully grasp, more fully understand and treasure these and His other bountiful gifts and blessings.

Our dearest Lord is at this very moment here in our midst! What a great blessing! What a blessed understanding! What a fabulous way to acknowledge the sacred, blessed and holy right here in my presence and right in the middle of a busy day. I more clearly understand that our dear Lord walks with me and others as one might be driving home from work, or one is finishing up working in the garden or in the fields. What a great blessing our dear Lord truly is! Blessed is He who comes in the Holy Name of our Lord! And blessed are we whose daily lives are but unfolding stories of the holy amid the ordinary, the Divine amid the human and Divine Love in union with human imperfection. It is a pure and unearned blessing to more fully see, understand and stand in awe as we faithfully grasp the ancient truth that indeed our Greatest Creator is walking in our company. Daily our good Lord blesses His beloved daughters and sons, all of them being holy, sacred and precious members of the imperfect, broken and frail human race. Lord, thank you for Your countless blessings on me and all humanity. Holy is Your Name, O Lord, our God. AMEN.

March 15, 2020

WHY FAITH DOES MATTER

"'Did I not tell you that if you believe you will see the glory of God?' So they took away the stone. And Jesus raised his eyes and said, 'Father, I thank you for hearing me. I know that you always hear me; but because of the crowd here I have said this, that they may believe that you sent me" (John 11:40–42). In this time when the coronavirus is striking great fears throughout the world, we can allow this modern pandemic to pierce our daily lives and we can surrender to our fears. Or, we can certainly live our daily lives in very responsible ways. First, we take whatever precautionary steps we must take to protect our daily lives, that of our children and other family members.

As modern disciples of Christ, now is a time when we ought to go down the street and check on our neighbors—especially the elderly, those whose health is frail, and also our neighbors whose names we might not even know. As children of God when we are confronted by serious health issues, human suffering and even death, the last thing we do is bury our head in the ground! This is a very historical time when our own national, state and local political leaders, our religious leaders, our educators, our major corporate leaders and other leaders tell us it is paramount that we stay away from others. I say to you, we are NOT to be irresponsible or negligent in the ways we respond to this very serious, evenly deadly coronavirus. But, we are NOT hermits. No. We can imitate Christ when he walked into the presence of the deceased Lazarus and his depressed sisters, and the doubting crowd, and Jesus used his infinite faith to transform death into new life.

Today your faith, my faith, can enable us to take this historic time of serious health challenges and use it as a time to extend our genuine concern, care and compassion toward others. I hope we freely and willingly and in responsible ways allow the Gospel message of Christ and our modern discipleship to be our main choice of just HOW we approach these times. Or, do we allow fear, ignorance and indifference to be our choices? Each of us must make these decisions. I pray that Christ's great faith, his love for Lazarus and the fullness of his trust in his Father will be the way you might choose to imitate as we approach this current challenge. Each of us will make our choices. Be prudent. Be informed. May we strive to safely and carefully imitate Christ.

March 22, 2020

LAZARUS
AND YOU

Lazarus was a man whose life was filled with daily suffering. His sisters, Martha and Mary, deeply loved Him. A man like Lazarus in our modern society all too often is relegated to some obscure place in society. All too often, in our modern society, a modern Lazarus is seen as being a burden on family and friends. Ironically, and very, very often the modern suffering man or woman is welcomed into the lives of others whose own frailties and suffering have produced in them immense qualities such as, but certainly not limited to, endurance, determination, courage, perseverance, greater knowledge, greater understanding and greater wisdom of the heart.

When you or someone in your family or a neighbor, a work associate or even a stranger enters your life, you and others will quietly take stock, observe and recognize that this young man or woman, even a boy or girl has a way about themselves that is well beyond the expected levels of maturity, understanding and even wisdom. Suffering can produce perseverance, endurance and courage. Suffering can create a deep sadness. Whoever is a modern Lazarus needs to choose which way to live out this one lifetime. Will suffering manage them or will they manage suffering? Will more misery come out of their suffering or will their suffering produce greater goodness? All of us are simple, broken and imperfect frail human beings.

We all witness others' suffering. All of us experience suffering. Trust like Lazarus. Stay close to our good Lord. Understand that the misery of the Cross was followed by the renewal and new life in the Risen Christ. If you are suffering, pray. If you witness suffering, pray. In prayer, close your eyes, open your heart, mind, and spirit, and allow our beloved Lord to create in you a new person…a person who gives away the Light of Christ, the Hope needed to awaken through a breaking dawn and witness the gift of His New Day and New Life in Christ. Make your choices like Lazarus. Be steadfast like Martha and Mary. In your heart prepare, sustain and welcome our dear Lord. And know He is with you now, through it all and until the holy hour of your death. Know this, and in your own brokenness be humbled. And may we give thanks to our Lord. AMEN.

March 29, 2020

SUFFERING

"Do not neglect hospitality, for through it some have unknowingly entertained angels" (Heb. 13:2). That stranger in your midst is a human being and thus a man, woman or child who already is sacred, precious and holy. Our dear Lord sent forth His only begotten Son to teach and preach, forgive and heal, and to die and rise in fulfillment of the ancient prophets. Why would God send forth His beloved Holy Child? God so loved the world and chose to send into our world a Savior long sought by countless human beings.

Now today, as we celebrate Divine mercy, let us be or become people of humble heart, people whose daily lives force us to acknowledge our own deep and frustrating limitations, frailties and broken human nature. Fear not suffering. Fear not death. Fear nothing. Rather, in these historical days of growing severe international suffering and daily increases in deaths, may each one of us take time daily to be people of deep and humble gratitude. Suffering is all around us. It is often within one's own life and the lives of family members, friends, neighbors and many strangers. St. Mother Teresa of Calcutta wrote, "Pain and suffering have to come into your life, but remember pain, sorrow, suffering are but the kiss of Jesus—a sign that you have come so close to Him that He can kiss you."

Human suffering, daily lives lived with hearts deeply embedded in faith, and lives lived with a brutal, yet humbling frankness and honesty, are all burdens borne by countless people. We owe ourselves truth. We can never achieve the entire fullness of truth. Our mind, heart and spirit are but limited in nature. The fullness of truth can only be sought when countless people join together and seek truth, greater knowledge, greater understanding and a greater fullness of truth. Together, as we suffer, we can make it. By ourselves, all we will have is wishful thinking, a fool's truth, and ultimately failure. However, together, as members of our one common human nature, we can rediscover the fullness of humanity and its great gifts of courage, humility, perseverance, determination, tenacity, grit, wonderment, greater knowledge, greater understanding, greater faith, greater hope, and greater love. You are not in this world by yourself, you never were or ever will be. Amid our suffering may we be courageous and humbled enough to make time to look, see and rediscover Christ in the lives of those who are suffering, amid the daily lives of the poor, and in the lives of frail and simple people. There is a great dignity in the lives of those who experience suffering.

May we be humbled to rediscover that our dear Christ enters our daily lives as we cross paths with the ill, suffering or dying. Without His death, Christ could not have experienced His Resurrection. May we imitate Christ by experiencing this ongoing suffering and rediscovering the New Life we can obtain through Christ. God so loved the world that He sent forth His only begotten Son. St. Pope John Paul II who suffered and died from Parkinson's disease wrote, "Those who share in the sufferings of Christ are also called, through their own sufferings, to share in glory." Divine mercy will always triumph over suffering and death. May we continue to rediscover the fullness, beauty, and courage firmly rooted in our ancient faith. AMEN.

April 19, 2020

ON THE ROAD TO CHRIST

Looking back on my own lifelong journey to draw closer to our Savior Jesus Christ, I decided to pray about, and reflect on these six decades plus of life I have been able to experience. My life has been and remains my ongoing personal "Road to Emmaus" story. Luke's story about these ancient disciples of Christ reflect far too many times in my life when I went from believing to questioning to wavering to doubting to walking away and then back into the company of Christ. In a lifelong search for Christ, it is fine, it is required for a believer to question, search for greater understanding, and ultimately to seek a greater fullness of Truth—the eternal Truth brought to fulfillment by the Risen Christ. This ancient story found in Luke's Gospel is known as "The Road to Emmaus." It is my story, your unfolding story, and that of billions of lives around the modern world. Seek Truth. This you owe to yourself!

The following is a prayer I wrote around 6 a.m. on Thursday, April 16, 2020. It's a very brief heartfelt and prayerful description of my ongoing relationship with our dear Lord.

Dear Lord, I am not certain how or where I am to go in this one unearned lifetime. I give You my whole being, my heart, my mind, and my spirit. I cannot know for certain where I will be tomorrow; or how I will journey there. I cannot know whom I shall meet. I cannot know why our paths shall cross. However, my Lord and my God, I know this day and forever that You are my God in whose Divine company I shall forever strive to walk humbly, to love goodness and to serve others. AMEN.

For I know well the plans I have for you...to give you a future of hope.

(Jer. 29:11)

Michael Briese

Somewhere within you is a heart afire! It is a heart, in fact, a sacred vessel, and a temple in which our dear Lord now rests. When life or circumstances burden you, when worries dominate your thoughts, or when your faith seems weak, be willing to quiet down, and with the trust of a child, ask our dear Lord to watch over you, guide you, and enter more fully into your very being. On that ancient Road to Emmaus two broken hearts and doubting minds were restored and brought to new life…a NEW LIFE spent in the company of Christ. Go out into your part of society and seek and find our dear Lord. Look and you will see Him. Listen and you will hear our Lord speaking to you. In silence, wonder and you will find wisdom. Pray and you will see God. AMEN.

April 26, 2020

VOICE OF THE SHEPHERD

Then God led forth His people like sheep, guided them like a flock through the wilderness. He led them on secure and unafraid. (Ps. 78:52–53)

Because of the Shepherd, the Rock of Israel. (Gen. 49:24)

For he is our God, we are the people he shepherds, the sheep in his hands. (Ps. 95:7)

For I know well the plans I have in mind for you...to give you a future of hope. (Jer. 29:11) May mercy, peace, and love be yours in abundance. (Jude 2)

The previous Scripture verses express the abundant harvest waiting for you, me and all who truly seek our dear Lord. No obstacle can obstruct your relationship with our Lord other than a closed mind or a closed heart. No government, no military might, no powerful billionaire can prevent you from growing in your faith, in your hope and in your love for God. No power can do this! None at all!

Hear the ancient Voice of our Lord. Listen. Make time to pray. Go off to a quiet place and just breathe, be still, and in that momentary silence, ask our dear Lord to come closer and to enter more fully into the very depth of your being. Unlike McDonald's this is NOT like a fast-food process. This spiritual journey is daily, ongoing and need not end until you draw your last breath. Then, after a faithful life, you will be blessed with eternal life resting in the company of Christ. But wait!

You are very much alive! You can witness the brightly shining sun rays that permeate the heavens as each dawn breaks. You can listen as the birds sing amid the breaking day. You can smell the sweet flowers all around you.

You can touch the soft fur of your own God-created pet. You enjoy your mobility as you depart from your privilege of having your own place to call home. Therein you have food in the refrigerator, clothes in the closets, electricity, air-conditioning and heat, and pictures to remind you about memorable people and events. You are so richly blessed in many ways.

Our Good Shepherd's Holy Voice echoes ever so quietly within the very depths of you. In this one lifetime, make a serious lifelong effort to discover, pursue and more fully understand our Lord. He is our Good Shepherd whose Voice enlightens hearts and minds. Seek the fullness of Truth through Christ. Or you, like all too many, can search for truth through the likes of government, industry, technology, science and other great fields of study. But TRUTH rests within you. *Seek and you will find. Knock and the door will be opened. Ask and it shall be given.* Also, become a forgiver, let go of the past, and love even those you might not like...including your enemy. Do this and throughout this wholly unearned God-given gift of one lifetime, always choose to run this lifelong race in the company of Christ. Listen to your heart for the heart has reasons the mind knows not. Last, over your lifetime strive to love our dear Lord with all your heart, all your mind and all your spirit. May peace be with you. AMEN.

May 3, 2020

WHERE ARE YOU GOING?

Jesus said, "Where [I] am going you know the way." Thomas said to him, "Master, we do not know where you are going; how can we know the way?" Jesus said to him, "I am the way and the truth and the life. No one comes to the Father except through me." (John 14:5–6). Where are YOU going in life? How are you going there? Why are you going there? Who are you looking for? What are you trying to accomplish? The ancient Greek philosopher, Socrates wrote, "The unexamined life is not worth living." When St. Thomas asked his question, Jesus already knew that Thomas's heart was indeed afire and in search of something greater, some more thorough understanding as to why Thomas was even on earth; and last, Thomas, though filled with doubts and questions, was also blessed with faith, hope and love. Thomas could be you, me or any person.

Open your heart, mind and spirit to the Gospel. You need not be or become some great fan of the Bible. You need not be or become a Church hopper. You need not become some self-righteous person you are not. Rather, our dearest Lord and Savior Jesus Christ looks right inside you. He knows you better than you ever will know yourself. He sees all your good and beauty and He sees your frailties and weaknesses. Truth is Truth! And you owe yourself one lifetime in which you daily realize you owe yourself Truth. Open your very being to God and all His infinite Divine mercy, wisdom and love. Become that very person our Creator calls you to become. Be not in a hurry. It will require your whole lifetime. Be patient, but persist!

Strive throughout the passing of each hour every day for the rest of your life to walk humbly, to bear any sorrows and to courageously confront brutal truths. Also, dare to ask our Lord for the abilities needed to surrender your life and your entire being to our very Creator who formed you in His ways and granted you this one lifetime. Give up your own wants, desires and dreams. Rather, do not seek gold, power or fame. Instead, be willing to possess little or nothing in materials and instead to discover, rediscover and become divinely blessed with a fortune contained within the blessed heart only God can grant you. There within the silence of your very being you will come to know God and God will know you. When a man or woman humbly gives everything away, he or she ironically is blessed many times over with an infinite treasure that only God can inspire, nurture and bring to greater fruition.

Thomas with all his doubts chose to persevere in the company of Christ. Twenty-one centuries later, Thomas and his doubts remain famous, even historical. Thomas is you and me with all our questions. Thomas and his great faith and holy life is a clear reminder to us: That our dear Lord invites us to come closer and to draw near to Him. May we have the courage and audacity needed to spend a lifetime in the company of Christ. It is always better to be a fool for Christ, than a "foolish wise man!" AMEN.

May 10, 2020

YOUR SPIRITUAL CAREER PATH

Jesus said to his disciples: "If you love me, you will keep my commandments. And I will ask the Father, and he will give you another Advocate to be with you always, the Spirit of truth, which the world cannot accept, because it neither sees nor knows it. But you know it, because it remains with you, and will be in you." (John 14:15–17)

Because you were conceived and delivered into this world, and because you are now breathing and are consciously aware of your own self and your very being, you are proof that God loves. Your own one life is precisely because God willed your very being, your very life and your very essence. Your life is pure gift; an unearned and unmerited gift from God. Your life and the life of every single human being is from its very conception a life created by our Father who art in heaven. As such, your life and that of all our brothers and sisters are holy lives, sacred lives and precious lives. God did this! Why?

What did you do to deserve God's immense love and this one gift of life? Did you earn God's love and this life He breathed into the very depth of your very being? Why would God love you, me or any human being? Look at our human history. All throughout, the human race has oppressed, murdered, tortured, beaten, assaulted, raped and robbed one another. Why? Who knows just how many wars we have fought in our ongoing efforts to use the weaponry we create to wound, maim, kill and then oppress our fellow human beings? Why? Why does God so love us that He sent forth His only begotten Son to walk among us? Why would God do this?

You have today, this very moment. You know not whether you will have tomorrow. As far as yesterday goes, it never comes back. Never! Hold no hatred, animosity or desire for vengeance within the very depth of your

God-given being. Forgive those who trespass against you. Love your enemies even those who hate you. Give unto others with no conditions attached. That breath you just took was given unto you by God with no conditions attached. Imitate Christ.

Seek Truth throughout this one lifetime. Worry not one bit about what others might think about you. Remain Christ-centered. Worry not about tomorrow. Live this holy moment and holy hour now. If tomorrow is meant for you, then, be assured, our Lord will awaken you amid the breaking of the new tomorrow. Like today, tomorrow will be a holy day precisely because it will always be another day our dear Lord has made and will grant unto all of us. Where is your own spiritual career path taking you today? Journey forth in the ways our dear Lord asks you to pursue. Listen in prayer to the Holy Spirit. Waste not a moment. Each minute passes like a fleeting mini-second! Here now, then gone forever. Seek God. Love God. Love our dear Lord with all your heart, all your mind and all your spirit. Do this in the Holy Name of our Lord and Savior Jesus Christ.

Then, when years have passed and age has settled in on you, take some time and look back, and see just how much you faithfully sought to live your life in the company of Christ. Where will your spiritual career path take you? You cannot know for many years. But today, be and more fully become a modern disciple of Christ. Then, when the sunset of your life has arrived, allow your heart to more fully grasp the outstretched hands of our Lord. Allow Him to welcome you into His eternal company. There, in His company, shall you be granted the fullness of eternal life, eternal rest and eternal peace. AMEN.

May 17, 2020

A BEGGAR'S CUP

In "The Agony in the Garden," Saint Luke writes: "Then going out he went, as was his custom, to the Mount of Olives, and the disciples followed him. When he arrived at the place he said to them, "Pray that you may not undergo the test." After withdrawing about a stone's throw from them and kneeling, he prayed, saying, "Father, if you are willing, take this cup away from me; still, not my will but yours be done." [And to strengthen him an angel from heaven appeared to him. He was in such agony and he prayed so fervently that his sweat became like drops of blood falling on the ground.] When he rose from prayer and returned to his disciples, he found them sleeping from grief. He said to them, "Why are you sleeping? Get up and pray

that you may not undergo the test."
(Luke: 22:39–46)

If you are reading these words, then you already understand that Jesus Christ was no ordinary man who did some extraordinary things. Rather, Christ came because he followed the will of his Father who art in heaven. Christ did not do what he wanted to do. Instead he made time and went out with his closest friends to do nothing but pray. Prayer is the language of the human heart. Prayer is the language in which the Holy Spirit might whisper, groan or even sing in words that God Himself scripted. Together within the very depth of your being, deep within the protected sacred shelter of the human heart rests our Risen Savior Jesus Christ.

Right within you rests the company of the sacred, precious and holy ones. Have you ventured into the very depth of your being? Have you gone away from actions and simply discovered stillness, silence and the great harvests such grace-filled actions can have on one young person? Christ is here, right there within the very depth of your sacred being.

Michael Briese

Go there! Pray there. End a day there and begin each new day with raised hands, a bowed head, and then humbly rediscover that indeed our dear Lord is with you, now and until the hour of your death.

June 02, 2020

MOST HOLY TRINITY

For God so loved the world that he gave his only Son, so that everyone who believes in him might not perish but might have eternal life. For God did not send his Son into the world to condemn the world, but that the world might be saved through him. Whoever believes in him will not be condemned, but whoever does not believe has already been condemned, because he has not believed in the name of the only Son of God. (John 3:16–18)

It is written in the Book of Genesis that one evening Adam and Eve were walking along in the Garden of Eden. They were still very close to God. They had not yet eaten from that forbidden apple. They knew within the very depths of their being that God was with them!

They heard our dear Creator as He whispered to them as softly as a soft breeze. They both heard our dear God precisely because they had consistently and freely chosen to live their daily lives in accordance with God's ways. How do you now choose to live out your daily life? Is it in the ways of Christ? Is it in accordance with the wisdom of the Holy Spirit? How do you live out your one pure unearned gift of human life?

In the ancient Catholic Tradition, we can discover an old term used to describe the Most Holy Trinity. The Trinity is the Triune Oneness of the Divine: Father, Son and Holy Spirit. If we need proof of this Divine relationship, then open your heart, mind and spirit and understand that you are alive with your gift of one life because through the love of your father and mother, you were conceived and born into this world. Your own life results in a triune oneness of humanity present in you. You are partially the presence of your mother and the presence of your father. You are the new creation. In you is a human triune…an image of the Divine Triune Oneness. Just as God is love, so too are you and every human being called to love.

At the moment of your birth, a new life was granted a place, a role and a divinely inspired purpose here in God's creation. In today's world, we do not walk in that ancient land known as the Garden of Eden. In today's society, it is way too easy to be tempted and to fall to temptation after temptation. St. John writes, "For God so loved the world that he gave his only Son" (John 3:16). Our ancient Faith assures us that like the Risen Christ, the Son of God, we too shall die and are invited by our dear Lord to rise into the Eternal Life Christ obtained for us. This infinite Divine love is unconditional love. It exemplifies Divine gifts such as mercy, justice, compassion, forgiveness and love. In this one lifetime know our Triune Oneness of the Divine has been with you since your conception. Know the holiness of our Lord rests within you. Know our Lord avails His gift of life to you, His humble holy child through every breath God grants you. May you go forth this very hour knowing our Lord is with you, now and until the hour of your death. AMEN.

June 7, 2020

HATE OR LOVE

The choices are yours to make all throughout your God-bestowed lifetime. Dr. Martin Luther King Jr wrote, "Hate begets hate; violence begets violence; toughness begets a greater toughness. We must meet the forces of hate with the power of love... Darkness cannot drive out darkness; only light can do that. Hate cannot drive out hate; only love can do that."

How can one recognize true love? "Love is when you had the courage and will to take that risk. It might have cost you your life, every ounce of sinew and every beat of your heart! You took that risk, opened your heart, surrendered your own self and even risked a broken heart. From the very start, God, you and our fellow brothers and sisters were meant to become a union of love; a union of new life and one of many blessings unto all."

Maybe we might freely choose to step back, quiet down and say this or a similar thought: "Dear Lord, I am not certain how or where I am to go in this one unearned lifetime. I give you my whole being, my heart, my mind and my spirit. I cannot know for certain where I will be tomorrow, or how I will journey there. I cannot know who I shall meet. I cannot know why our paths shall cross. However, my Lord and my God, I know this day and forever, that You are my God in whose Divine company I forever shall strive to walk humbly, to love goodness and to serve others." Or we might say, "Lord, I ask You, dear Creator, to take my heart, my mind, my spirit and my entire being and create in me the new person, the better person and the more compassionate and just person, You, dear Lord call me to become."

If peace is to prevail over hatred, then we have to learn to love others, including people we do not like or want to be around. The dignity of every human being is not based on one's asset–liability ratio. Rather, your greatest treasure was planted and given unto you months before you were born. Use whatever time, talents and skills you have to help renew and strengthen our communities. Last, strive to be at peace with oneself, family, the strangers and God. In short, live in a right manner in which you honestly can love others. Love is your greatest power. Use it. The choice is always yours to make, "Do I want to hate or love?" What is your answer to this profound question? If you are not certain, then ask, "What would Christ do?" Peace.

June 14, 2020

BE NOT AFRAID

Like a mighty champion: my persecutors will stumble, they will not prevail. In their failure they will be put to utter shame, to lasting, unforgettable confusion. Lord of hosts, you test the just, you see mind and heart, Let me see the vengeance you take on them, for to you I have entrusted my cause. Sing to the Lord, praise the Lord, For he has rescued the life of the poor from the power of the evildoers! (Jer. 20:10–13)

Be not afraid! Fear not the insults, threats or denunciations others will throw at you. Let them talk behind your back. Let them utter every insult they can think up. Your own life and that of every human being is pure gift. Even those who insult you, betray you or manipulate you are human beings. They are your brothers and sisters. Sadly, all too often, the deep yearning, thirst or heartfelt desire for peace, purpose or self-acceptance is denied to some people. They want to have what their neighbor or relative might possess. They might desire the status, power or influence another person might have. Or, maybe they simply do not like their own self. Whatever the cause or root of their misery might be, our dear and beloved Lord calls you, me and all who freely choose to walk in His footsteps to respect, accept and forgive those who trespass against us. No exceptions to this edict expressed by Christ.

Be not afraid of those who might use their fame, fortune or power to assault your character, reputation or daily efforts. Unless you are running for public office, there is but one very important voter whose strong support you truly desire— our Lord and Savior Jesus Christ. If you can allow others to speak down about you, cast lies and innuendos, and even strive to defame you. Then, and only then, will you truly obtain the graces, blessings, courage, perseverance and steadfast faith needed to rise from the ashes of defeat. One by one and over time pick up a solid stone and rebuild your own life…a life of blessed and humbling daily discipleship, a daily way of living through service unto the least among us and a life deeply rooted in your deep abiding love for our Crucified and Risen Lord and Savior Jesus Christ.

Insults are nothing more than syllables brought together to form words, and words are connected in thoughts and another's thoughts can be callous, indifferent and very insulting. Nonetheless words are hot air coming out of one's mouth. When these pieces and sounds of words are vexations, then, you freely, knowingly and willingly ask our dear Lord to enable you to receive, put aside and ignore such hostile, insulting or threatening words.

Be not afraid! Rather, in prayer, deep within the very depth of your being you will discover and rediscover the holy presence of our dear Lord Jesus Christ. Christ will always prevail over human insults and hot air. Give your haters the forgiveness, mercy and love God gave to you. Do this throughout your finite lifetime. In the end, when the angels of the Lord come into your company to bring you closer and into the company of our dear Savior, you can know with full certitude that you did the best you could do. Sure you failed at times. But success was yours for the asking.

Our Lord hears your prayerful cries and grants you a lifetime filled with countless blessings, greater faith, greater hope and greater love. Be humbled by such Divine mercy. Never let human words and vexation distance you from Christ. Forgive those whose words hurt you. Do not return hatred with hatred.

Be not afraid! Rather, be willing to love those who might not even like you. In the end, you will have given this unearned God-given gift of life your best. This is what our Lord asks from all of us: Forgive those who trespass against you and let go of the past. Peace.

June 21, 2020

FEAR NOT GENUINE DOUBTS OR QUESTIONS OF THE SPIRITUAL NIGHT

Jesus said to the Twelve, "Therefore do not be afraid of them. Nothing is concealed that will not be revealed, nor secret that will not be known. What I say to you in darkness, speak in the light; what you hear whispered, proclaim on the housetops." (Matt. 10:26–27)

Fear is the greatest power that can conquer a human being's heart, mind and spirit. Very often hatred is deeply embedded in fear. As a result of that fear, one distances him- or herself from "those people," "those communities" or "those organizations." All of "those other ones" all too often are made up of people who might not be people of one's own "group." Often "those other ones" belong to different groups of race, sexual orientation, political affiliation, religious faiths, commercial groups, labor organizations, social leanings or one or more of "those other group" categories. Well, you and I are but one kind of human being. We share a common nature—a human nature—a nature with only two natural and major distinct groups: men and women. Both are the image and likeness of our one common Creator.

Long ago God breathed life into the first members of our one common thread—our common human nature. Since then powerful forces, be they empires, armies, oppressors and even horrendous and evil human beings, have truly developed far too many categories to define and divide various peoples. We are one common human race! There is no other human race! We are it!

All too often a man or woman has the audacity within the very depths of their being to actually subscribe, accept or believe the idea that one group of people is better than or superior to other groups. Or they might believe "their own group" is "the one true group" in total contradiction to the reality that all such group labels are man-made group labels. Please take a step back. Please!

When one accepts such generalizations or stereotypes as being truths, we have a very serious problem. If you believe this way, you have willingly or maybe unknowingly subscribed and maybe even accepted that you are superior to another human being. Certainly people are superior in their fields of work, sports or professions. Nonetheless every single person on Earth is of our one common human nature. We all witness each sun setting, while darkness has begun to set in, and the darkness of night completely envelops our entire nature. All people must submit to time…God's time. Amid the darkness of night, as silence permeates the air, take a moment to realize just how frail, vulnerable and limited you truly are. And so too is every other man, woman or child.

Like Christ, be willing to serve others. Be willing to sacrifice. Be willing to love people you do not like. Be humble enough to recognize Christ in the eyes of the beggar at the local market. Be attentive, watch for Christ and you will repeatedly discover Him. You have heard the Word of God. You have been drawn closer to our Lord. You have chosen to find rest and stillness in the company of our dear Lord and with many others, whose hearts, like your own, are afire with their love for Christ.

Run your lifelong race willing to serve Christ by meeting men, women and children right where they are in this life. Also, pray, trust and believe our dear Lord speaks to them through your own blessed faith, hope and love. Go out in this world and be not afraid. Our Lord is always with us. Jesus said, "Everyone who acknowledges me before others I will acknowledge before my heavenly Father" (Matt. 10:32). Come closer and make time to find rest, stillness and peace in the company of Christ. Do this and you will come to discover greater faith, greater hope and greater love. Last, listen, as Jesus would say, "Do this in memory of Me" (Luke 22:19). AMEN.

June 28, 2020

PRAYER FOR THE HOMELESS

This day is a pure gift from God. All human life is a pure gift from God. Every passing hour is a pure unearned gift from God. Our food, clothing and housing are gifts from God. Our one common human nature is the most important God-given gift each and every person possesses. Every man, woman and child is our brother and sister. Our dear Lord was born in a shack. Jesus was brought into this world as a homeless baby with no stable housing. He was born with only the clothing wrapped around his holy body. He had nowhere to rest his head without the kindness and charity of others. This Holy Child was born poor because in his poverty he possessed immense blessings. When you see a poor person, you are looking at the image of our poor Savior. You are witnessing an image in whose face and quivering voice you can see and hear the cries of those in need. When a man, woman or child asks or begs you to be charitable, that is the Christ Child. They are not merely "poor"—they also exemplify the poor Christ, our poor Savior whose greatest wealth was and remains his infinite love.

Dear Lord and Savior Jesus Christ, we come before you and in our poverty of heart we beg you to enrich our goodness, our yearning to serve rather than be served, and our willingness to generously give unto our needy brothers and sisters. We hunger for You, dear Lord.

July 25, 2020

PRAYER OF A BEGGAR

Lord, I am a beggar whose impoverished heart is poor in spirit, whose mind begs for greater faith, hope and love and whose body cries out in its own suffering. Lord, I have no other friend or neighbor like You. Lord, I beg You, please enable me to get beyond my poverty of love. Enable me to see You in the lives of the poor. Come dear Lord, and please, may I, as a mere beggar, cry out and ask You to enrich my life with a heart of gold, and a deep abiding heartfelt desire to enter into the impoverished lives of my fellow human beings. My dear Lord, enable my eyes to see You, my ears to hear You and my heart to be thankful when I enter into the life of a poor man, woman or child. There in the lives of the poor, I discover and rediscover You, O Lord, my God. Holy are You, dear Lord of the poor! AMEN.

July 25, 2020

DOWN ON MY KNEES

Late one morning, as I walked the winding paths of a beautiful park, I came upon a man doing some serious gardening. I watched him for a few minutes. Then I asked this old gardener why he cared so much for these plants. He smiled upon hearing my question and said, "I get down on my knees because I understand I am here but for a short time. I am the steward of this part of God's creation. As I pull weeds, plant seeds and prune the bushes, I give thanks to our dear beloved Creator. I give thanks to our Lord for the countless species of plant life He has bestowed upon humanity. He gave me my hands, the very hands I use to help produce new life by planting, caring for and sustaining the new life in this new generation of plant life. I am an old gardener. I am a simple man. I love our dear Lord because our Lord loves humanity so much that He has granted us a great worldwide mosaic garden of life. Where I go, the hands of our Lord are there. Here I am, down on my knees, praying in a spirit of awe and gratitude. And I fully understand this is precisely why I am down on my knees. I hope this answers your question." I just stood there amazed.

God spoke to me that moment in my life. It was a day long ago…a day from which I learned. Now, I find myself down on my knees tending the garden God gave me. I humbly accept the Lord's invitation to draw near, to enter into prayer more fully, and to truly understand that I am down on my knees as a humble steward with a place, a purpose and a role to play in the unfolding of God's Kingdom here at hand. Like that old gardener, I, too, am down on my knees and am blessed with a deep abiding spirit of thanksgiving, joy and deep heartfelt awe. Down on my knees, I am at once stunned and forever humbled by our one Divine Gardener. And I, a mere laborer for the Lord in His Garden of Love, give thanks to You, O Lord, my God. AMEN.

July 27, 2020

A PRAYERFUL DREAM

My Lord, my God, I come to You in prayer. I come before You dreaming that one day…

My life will become a life deeply rooted in the holiness of Your beloved Son, our Savior Jesus Christ.

My prayerful heartfelt cries will help me in my daily efforts to more fully understand You, our dearly beloved Father, who art in heaven.

My life will continue for countless days and years to be and become a life centered ever more fully on the holy life lived out by Your Holy Child whose Sacred Heart assures me that my daily life is sustained by Your Divine mercy and justice.

My heartfelt desire to serve You, oh Lord, is, in fact, a reflection of Your Divine invitation to me and countless others to come closer into Your company and, in Your Divine presence, discover and rediscover the truth of Your deep and abiding Divine love.

My prayerful dream reminds me that my humanity and its immense imperfections, brokenness, frailties and gifts are now, and can ever more clearly become, Your blessings in disguise.

My dear Lord, how am I to know when You are in my presence? What am I to look for to find You, see You or hear You? I ask in humble words and thoughts. I cannot answer my questions. Will You please enter more fully into my quiet, prayerful heart and grant unto me Your Divine, heartfelt wisdom?

My God, I can dream about a better life for me, my loved ones and society. I pray for this. However, just how am I, in accord with Your will to contribute to improving and sustaining our common good and the renewal and building up of Your kingdom here at hand?

My Lord and my God, please send forth Your Holy Spirit and Your countless blessings. Please open up hearts, minds and spirits. Allow Your Divine wisdom to bring peace among enemies, healing to broken hearts, reconciliation among family members and genuine mutual respect and acceptance by various peoples. Last, I beg You, my God, to grant unto me greater faith, greater hope and greater love.

My life is in its evening. The high noon sun has come and gone. The setting of this passing day and my life inspire me to look up toward the heavens and all I can claim is my own deep heartfelt awe of You. Your infinite Divine will grants me every breath I have ever taken, every passing minute and hour in which I have been blessed with life, the breaking of every new day, the abundant crops and the countless creatures of the vast oceans, mountains, plains, forests and skies. O God, You truly entered into a deep, abiding love relationship with humanity and have blessed us time and again.

YOU ARE MY LORD AND GOD. THANKS BE TO YOU, O LORD, MY GOD.

July 28, 2020

THE POOR ARE US

People associate poverty and being poor with economic poverty. That is to say, a rich man who is financially wealthy is better than a poor man who owns little of any real financial value. Well, there are different kinds of poverty. There certainly is a diversity of the poverty experienced by members of our one common human race. There is little or no mystery as to why every year very successful men and women who are famous athletes, movie stars, musicians and leaders in others fields kill themselves. For all their external wealth or fame or power, they were empty inside. Many had turned for solace through the traditional modes, such as drugs, alcohol, daily pleasures at the expense of others, sexual promiscuity, gambling and the ancient modes of abuse of powers, influence and authority. This is simply to remind you, me and all people that right within you, your very being, rests the greatest treasure...a treasure planted within you at your sacred, precious and holy moment of conception, and sustained and brought into the unfolding of human history at your holy moment of birth. On that day, at that precious moment, God graced humanity with you. God blessed you with innate goodness, your one unearned life and countless breaths to sustain your life.

What do you give back to God, yourself and your countless brothers and sisters? This is a very important question you should ask, pray about, reflect on and frankly address as you wander through this one unfolding lifetime. Do you ever ask your self questions of wonderment, awe and greater understanding? Do you seriously pursue Truth? Wonder and you will find wisdom. Pray and you will see God. Seek Truth by making time to ask and address these innate questions of wonderment and about life. Strive to answer them with frankness and even brutal honesty.

Take the risk, and with courage be willing to open your heart to pains, injury, even brutal truths. Pain almost always precedes healing, strength and renewal. Be willing to lose your own life, trusting your new life, your new self and your new purpose will be followed with greater clarity and understanding. Be determined. Persevere. Never give up! With your own injuries learn about forgiveness, and grow in your abilities to grant pardon unto those who hurt you. Be willing to listen to unfavorable words, taunts or accusations, and still be willing to respect, love and serve these same people. Be willing to acknowledge your own brokenness. There amid your own frail, broken and imperfect self, you will come to discover God's ancient invaluable treasures resting within the very depths of your being. In the end, always choose to go with God.

Never give up. Pursue these basic heartfelt and intellectual questions throughout your one passing lifetime: Who am I? What is my purpose? When will I obtain greater understanding? Where am I going? Why am I here? How will I get there? Throughout your own lifetime only you can ask yourself and truthfully, even hope to answer these very ancient, personal and sacred questions. These fundamental questions, when asked, when seriously pursued, when honestly addressed and answered, can provide the cornerstones of your lifelong spiritual foundation. Seek and you will find Truth. Ask and it shall be given. You owe yourself Truth. Be well assured, if you are serious, many currently unknown men, women, and children will enter into your life and give unconditionally unto you, as you seek, pursue and strive to live out a life in search of greater understanding, meaning and purpose. The universe awaits you. Only you can live out this lifelong pursuit.

September 6, 2020